T0195922

The Child Inside

SUSAN LUKIN

Order this book online at www.trafford.com
or email orders@trafford.com

Most Trafford titles are also available at major online book retailers.

Print information available on the last page.

ISBN: 978-1-4907-6724-6 (sc)
ISBN: 978-1-4907-6723-9 (hc)
ISBN: 978-1-4907-6725-3 (e)

Library of Congress Control Number: 2015918999

Because of the dynamic nature of the Internet, any web addresses or links contained in
this book may have changed since publication and may no longer be valid. The views
expressed in this work are solely those of the author and do not necessarily reflect the
views of the publisher, and the publisher hereby disclaims any responsibility for them.

Any people depicted in stock imagery provided by Thinkstock are models,
and such images are being used for illustrative purposes only.
Certain stock imagery © Thinkstock.

Trafford rev. 12/09/2015

 www.trafford.com

North America & international
toll-free: 1 888 232 4444 (USA & Canada)
fax: 812 355 4082

Contents

Dedicated to my mother, father and two brothers,
my circle of love and encouragement.

I would like to acknowledge Rasheed Humphrey
for creating the cover illustration.

Introduction

To start to write a book about the subject of juvenile jail or juvenile detention…the forgotten, unwanted, ignored segment of a society, is not too hard when it has been lived every day. It is not difficult to call back memories, a sense of humanity and funny stories…and there are so many memories and unforgettable situations. What is hard is to realize and accept is the fact that many people don't really care about this segment of society. For many, it is just as well that it is not in view, put away, kept out of sight.

Life led me to take a path that has often been challenging, interesting and meandering along trails that have been overgrown with thorny brush…that have only been flattened and cleared with patience, tenacity and caring on the part of those staff members who work with the residents in detention. The life path was a walk into the juvenile detention system, which is usually thrown to the side by society. Society cannot really be blamed for not wanting to see its puzzling disappointments, its difficult children.

But, with a sigh of resignation, society knows that these children make up a segment of the whole, and this part of its own cannot be ignored and disowned. The children were created and nurtured by someone and now they have to be embraced by the rest of us. As much as we try to erase unpleasantness that we don't want to address, as much as we try to delete something, it seems to pop up again. Society might say, 'I got rid of that, I deleted it…I don't want to see it anymore'…but it re-appears like the click of a mouse, and the whole scenario is there, right in front of us again.

I want the click of the mouse to illuminate this segment of society so that others can see that it is not as bad as everyone thinks it is. Accept it or not, it is a part of us all. One thing we can do is to look at it in a different way, with a different perspective…a shift in thinking, feeling and acceptance. Another thing we can do is to realize that behind the walls of detention, there is a tremendous amount of humanity, of potential, of feeling, remorse, thought, consideration, loneliness, laughter and caring.

I want to delete the misconceptions, the misperceptions about this segment of society. What I have experienced can be shared. Maybe my experiences can be utilized to begin to change the view of an area that is generally ignored. After all, everyone keeps saying that the children are our future. No one has specified which children, where they live, what they look like, where they come from….

Asthma

So many of our residents have asthma. When I ask my boys if they have had any attacks since they came into detention, the majority say they have not, that they are not taking any medication and feel OK. Is it that they have been removed from the clouded, dusty air, away from hanging in the street, not having to look over their shoulders, not having to run from adversaries, to slip by bullets meant or not meant for them? Is it that they are away from family stress and pressures, away from knowing that they should be listening to mom, auntie or gram, but being too strongly pulled into doing what they know they are not supposed to be doing, finding some kind of fulfillment and approval from their friends?

Are they young and uncaring, knowing that they are not really being fulfilled, knowing that they are not really feeling themselves, not feeling their own pulses and heartbeats? Anxiety is caused by these frustrations and conflicts, of acting and knowing that they shouldn't really be acting that way, but doing it anyway….can it be that being removed from these stresses is allowing them to breathe a little freer? Their breath is no longer blocked as they are plunged against their will, into a new and different way of life.

When they come into detention, they come into a life and a system that is away from the car fumes of the urban way; away from dodging bullets; away from their being irresistibly drawn into a way of life they really know is not beneficial, but do it anyway; away from the love, but at times impatience with their mothers, knowing they should listen, but not listening; away from the taunting friends who often shame them into doing wrong things; away from the fast money; away from having to be the man of the house because their father is not and has not been there for a long time; very often away from an intact, caring family of wonderful people, who lost the fight against the lure of the streets; away from having to look and dress like everyone else, even though they don't have the money; away from being bunched together, doing as everyone else is doing, and not caring.

That is not to say that detention is a whole lot better. It has its own issues and stresses, but it is different from what they know, and that in itself is often a new start.

A New Start

A new start in detention. That sounds contradictory, but it is not necessarily so. In fact, detention is often a second chance in the young lives of our residents. Many, many boys have told me that if they had not come into detention, they would have been dead, the way many of their friends in the neighborhood wind up. Very often, they just verbalize these thoughts, but the longer they remain in detention, the more meaning those words have for them. This thought is reinforced by staff. I often bring to the residents another thought that many of the residents reject in the beginning of their stay: that even though they are in detention for something they may not have done, I ask if they have done things for which they have never gotten caught. If their answer to me is no, only they know the truth, but if their answer is a reluctant yes, I suggest that perhaps they are in detention to pay for the other things they did out there, even though this is not their official charge on the court papers. It's nice when they can begin to abstract and accept this reasoning.

I have always felt that the longer a resident remains with us in detention, the better off he is. As much as he wants to hit the streets again, as much as he misses his family, if he remains in detention, he will get a chance to grow while struggling with his frustrations, with the help of staff. Generally, his way of struggling with his frustration is to fight, to 'flip,' to 'wild out,' to be 'tight,' to resist his staff, to let fly whatever comes out of his mouth, to try to intimidate, to overturn furniture and to struggle against being restrained, cuffed and shackled. But the longer he stays, the more infrequent that behavior is manifested. He eventually finds it to be non-productive and he also finds himself on restriction. At last, the layers, as on an onion, begin to peel; the layers of the street, of the dusty, foul fumes, the survival, the running, dodging bullets, the needless waste, the life of not listening, not caring, callousness, guns, scars, not going to school, fast money, making babies, hanging out, getting high...begin to shrivel. Very slowly, they begin to curl back, unfolding, revealing the next layer of the street, the running, dodging, hanging...because this is learned for many years, in spite of the desires and hopes of his parents and relatives, of the school, of the more positive influences in his young life that attempt to counter his immersion in being bad. The aim is for us to drill down, discarding layer after layer, peeling back the call of the streets, to help him discover his own core, his own pulse and heartbeat.

Our residents are bombarded with all kinds of new spears of light in detention. They go to the Intake dormitory when they are admitted. Staff members speak to them from every Unit in the facility, including the Ombudsperson, the Chaplain, the school, the Medical and Mental Health staff, the Recreation staff and Case Management staff. For those new residents who are still quaking with rumors of detention that they heard when they were still 'in the world,' much of the information is probably lost, to be reabsorbed at a later time. For the repeaters, perhaps they will hear something they missed before or did not want to hear before, and realize that it was a truism that they should have heeded.

Each resident, new or old, goes through the routine of an admission physical, a mental health evaluation, an assessment to determine his school grades, and an Intake Interview by Case Management staff. Routines are explained to him. Expectations of behavior are stressed, but often are not absorbed and processed, which results in him acting out anyway. But he will run up against a constant wall of structure that he is not accustomed to. He will, as all children do, try to test this wall, often banging his head on the invisible wall of expectations and adult resistance. He won't win. His best choice is to listen to counseling and absorb it, utilize it and build with it and so the longer he remains with us in detention, the better off he is. The longer he stays, the more layers of the onion can have a chance to shrivel and peel back, revealing to himself his own inner core, his inner self.

Most of the residents in our detention facility are African-American and Hispanic. We have Asians on occasion, some Caucasians, Africans and Indian residents as well, and other nationalities round out the general population of the facility. How do the nationalities living so closely together relate to each other? I find that this seems to go in cycles. Much of the time, the residents get along, not even thinking of race or nationality. Other times, when issues, for some reason, seem to be more sensitive, we have more problems. During those times, the tensions swell in the dorms. The differences of shade, color, belief, background and other intangible variables that no one can really name, suddenly become very important. The desert sands shift in the wind, shimmer in the fading light, and carry on the business of being a desert, with no objection or interference. But if a grain of sand gets in someone's eye, the natural flow is interrupted. The eye ceases to function in its routine, well-lubricated way and the focus becomes the grain, which comes to feel like a stone in one's eye. When the irritant becomes a racial difference after that topic is insignificant for a long period of time, it becomes another topic of counseling for our residents, stressing the humanity of all, the melting pot of all of us. We are all the same.

How does a white person fit into all of this? For myself, it is not a question of fitting in; in fact, it has never been a question or topic of conversation as far as I have heard among the residents. But, I guess there is plenty to which I am not privy. One time, one of my residents had returned from Supreme Court after his remand date, and he was upset and very frustrated at how things had gone for him at his hearing. He was angry with everyone and was one to verbally express his feelings. He said, "That white judge! He's a loaf of Silvercup Bread!" This was a new expression for me. I told him if the judge is a loaf of Silvercup Bread, that makes me one too. He looked up surprised. He disagreed and said, "To me, you're Black and to the Spanish kids, you're Spanish."

That was one of the nicest compliments I have ever received.

Parents

I have the greatest respect for the parents of our residents. I meet most of them on visiting days when I am at the visiting desk, after they have placed all of their possessions in a small locker, only holding onto their two pieces of identification, going back and forth through the metal detector. At times, they come into the visiting area angry, hostile or crying, and at times, breathing hard and shallow, the sounds of asthma rasping through them, and I ask them if they are alright, if a glass of water would help. They often come straight from work, rushing to visit their child, still in their job uniforms, carrying a change of clean, fresh clothing on the subway so that their child can make a good court appearance before the judge.

They are parents who may be conditioned to expect a judgmental attitude from some, a disdain for their plight of having a son or daughter in detention. But they are parents who are struggling as much as anyone else to build a life, to love their children, and to try to provide a home life for them. They are, on the whole, nice people, who deserve attention, information and support as does anyone else. Even those who have not been able, for one reason or another, to provide the essentials, the nurturing and positive home life for the youth, deserve attention and respect. They may have fallen behind some of the others, but they deserve to be pulled along so that they can learn how to do what they might be fantasizing about....to live the American dream. They may not know how to grasp their fantasies and weave them into a tangible way of life, but maybe they can find a way to get there.

As angry and hostile as a parent is at times, and as ornery and disrespectful as he or she can be, one has to be that much more respectful, attentive and calm. After a while, the parent tends to become calm also, and hopefully becomes aware that the anger and mistrust are not necessary. Only then can sharing of information and communication begin. There are times, of course, that this approach doesn't work, which leads to taking a firmer, stronger approach with a visitor.

I have great respect for them, because they have been through more than most and they continue to go through this stressful experience, often to exhaustion. Although most have tried to guide their children, and care deeply for them, the drawing power of the streets and friends is too strong at an age when the youths do not yet have the knowledge and strength to resist. In other neighborhoods, the things that children learn on the streets may or may not be the same as our residents have experienced; but in most neighborhoods and households, most parents feel the same overwhelming shame and guilt when one of their offspring enters a criminal detention system.

I have met some wonderful, expressive, caring people who are the parents of our residents.

Afterwards

Very often, we wonder what happens to a youth when he leaves our facility, after he completes his time upstate and faces the streets again. The temptations remain the same, or are even worse for him. The same pull of the old life is staring at him, wanting to wrap its hands around him again. Many come back to our facility to say hello to staff; they have grown, and often have children of their own. They are proud to show us that they have made it and have resisted the old temptations and habits. Many return to us on new charges and they again go through the Orientation process and counseling that they did not want to hear before. I believe that the record of a resident returning to us as of this counting is sixteen times. In fact, he was one of mine and I greeted him each time with a 'welcome home.' Sometimes, we are all the structure they have.

For others, who fall in the eight, nine, ten, etc. admissions, I will ask if they want to break the record of sixteen, that we always have an available bed for him and he is always welcome back. He vigorously shakes his head no and says he is never coming back again. I answer that if he comes back, he should come back as staff, since he already knows the system from the inside out. One of my residents told me outright that his father was in jail, his grandfather had been in jail and he expected to carry on the family tradition.

At times, our 'graduates' get into more trouble upon their release. We hear through the 'network' when some of our former residents are killed, or have made the papers for more notorious charges, and it is sad for us to say that we tried to work with this one or that one and failed. When I hear of a former resident getting into more serious trouble, I wonder what more we could have done to prevent that from happening. At times, it is just meant to be, in that he comes back to learn the lesson he did not learn on his previous four, five or six etc. admissions. When I am asked how can I work with those youths who have done so many bad things, my answer is that I and others are here to try to keep them from doing those things again.

I feels very good to get a letter from a former resident who is attending college, and thanks me from the bottom of his heart for helping him, for being there for him while he was in detention.

He usually does not state what it is that I have done and most of the time, I don't know what it is that I have done, except to be there for him. One day, I was walking outside of the facility to the nearby post office and a car pulled up beside me. I man with a beard, in his twenties, whom I did not recognize, called out my name and seeing that I didn't recognize him, told me his name: a resident I had worked with in the facility. He thanked me for what I had done for him. I hadn't done anything special, but I graciously accepted the compliment and wished him continued favor.

Another time, a parent, now a community liaison, told me that in 2008, I was her son's Caseworker. She said that she and her son wanted to thank me for what I and a few other staff members had done for him. She told me his name, which I remembered, but I didn't remember what I had actually done. I was overwhelmed and speechless and almost became teary eyed. She said he was doing well and thanked me again. To touch another's life is such a humbling experience. Along with other staff, I am glad we were able to help him.

Recently, I was sitting at the visiting desk in the facility, processing visitors who came to visit their sons and daughters. A man came up to the desk and said that he was there to bring his younger brother clothing for his court appearance the following day. He said, 'I remember you. You were my Caseworker here when I was eleven. I was the smallest and youngest one on the dorm.' I looked at him trying to remember; there are so many residents who pass through our facility, but he looked vaguely familiar. I told him that I hoped he was doing well and asked if he had learned anything when he was with us; had we helped him? He shook his head slowly in remembrance and said, 'Definitely. I learned that I don't need anyone telling me what to do 24-7 and that I can do it on my own.' He said that he was now working in construction and doing well. He added, 'I also remember that you were kind to me.' What more can anyone ask for?

Each resident is riding on his own plane and at his own level. I am with each one wherever he is, trying to give him some strong ropes to grab onto, and we, the staff and I, begin the process of hauling him up. He scrapes himself on the protruding ledges along the way, getting bruised on outcrops or stumps of foliage that he has not experienced before, but always on an upward bend. I might not remember the specifics of what his charge was or what court he attended; I do remember holding onto the ropes, trying to help him heal wounds encountered along the way and letting him know that I and other staff won't get go of the ropes.

A Cauldron

Detention is a unique situation for adolescents. They are plucked from their natural and familiar environment of the city streets and are dropped into a giant cauldron, which is already bubbling and boiling with other residents' stories, problems, acting out and histories. Depending on how many times a child has been through the 'revolving door' of the detention and juvenile justice system, that is how high his anxiety level will be. Once he gets to know the routines of detention and the people who will be watching over him, he relaxes a little and may even enjoy his stay.

There are frequent emotional outbursts among both the boys and girls in detention if the particular personalities of a dormitory lend themselves to igniting one another. One incident occurred in a girls' dorm during a time of 'high tone' in the 'House.' A particular girl was having a hard time of it during that period and was either involved in or causing mayhem for a few minutes each day before the situation would be brought under control by staff. On one such day, her anxiety level was saturated and could absorb and tolerate no more. She started throwing things that probably should have been bolted to the floor. Yes, she actually lifted and threw over a large metal desk and an even larger bumper pool table. There was one saving grace that may show that some restraint was still left in her. Before she threw one particular desk, she stopped her tantrum, removed a number of plants that were on the desk, plus a lamp, and then continued her rampage.

She was escorted to the Medical Unit to ensure that she had not injured herself and a mental health referral was submitted. She apologized for her disruption and for her behavior. She was told to pick up what she had thrown, and she willingly obliged, since most of the time she was a rational girl. However, she was surprised when she could not budge the desk and pool table that she had flicked about in her time of anger.

The Nursery

The age of admission for boys and girls to come into detention in New York City is ten. Ten-year olds are infrequent visits to detention, but when they are picked up by the police and dropped off for their stay before they go to court, they can make a dormitory look like a nursery. They are usually very small compared to the other adolescents and evoke sympathy from the staff because they are so confused and they still cry easily. There are, of course, those ten-year olds who are terrors and they only evoke staff's frustration tolerance that is tested to its limits.

One of the confused little boys was a runaway from another agency and he was placed in detention one night until it could be determined the following day, where he belonged. He remembered one of the staff members from a previous admission, and he held the worker's hand like a little boy would hold the hand of his big brother or father.

We later learned, after he was returned to his placement, that he had taken pills. That was enough for us to shake our heads in sympathy for his confused life and we wondered about his future prospects. But, then we found out that the pills he had ingested were birth control pills and we had to laugh, compassion or not. I haven't done any research into what would happen to a male who takes female birth control pills, but the thought was enough to bring a laugh while we continued to shake our heads in sympathy.

The Staff of Life

Detention in New York City is similar to detention in many other cities and states. Freedom is curtailed; there is no wandering the building on the part of the residents; they are watched over by staff at all times; they line up and walk in a single file with their hands behind their backs when going to and from meals and other activities; they are not permitted to have in their possession money, pens or any unauthorized materials that are not provided by the facility; they are permitted no more than ten letters and ten pictures in their rooms; they are permitted only certain magazines and they are provided with one extra agency issued outfit which they can keep in their rooms. Anything else other than what is given to them by the agency is considered to be contraband.

There is not a corridor in the building that is not closed off and guarded by a locked, heavy steel door with an extra thick, fist-proof panel of unbreakable Plexiglas on some of the doors, that enables one to see who is on the other side of the door before opening it. Staff carries around a huge key on a ring that also sports other keys that are used for various functions around the facility. This key is the 'staff of life' in detention, since it is impossible to move around the building without it. At times, some residents may think about acquiring this key, but they are quickly reassured that it will get them nowhere. It is an interior key only, enabling staff to move within the building. A different key and a series of three controlled doors under the scrutiny of Security is required in order to exit the building.

One of the problems with this large key and the smaller keys jingling on its ring is what to do with it during the work day. The smaller keys open everything that a staff member needs to be opened and utilized: rest rooms, light switches, residents' rooms, closets, fire extinguisher boxes and offices. It is an intriguing issue since the key is somewhat cumbersome and heavy. Staff cannot put the keys down, since residents are always watching for an opportunity to do mischief. Some staff put the keys in their pockets, but they are heavy; some tuck the large key into a belt and leave the other keys jangling. Some try to wear the set of keys on a key chain or on a lanyard, but they are advised that this system leaves the staff member vulnerable. Most carry the keys in their hands until they feel like a permanent appendage. If the key is lost, the result is a deduction from a staff member's pay and one does not want to consider the consequences of the keys being found in the possession of a resident. But, that's another story.

After some time working in detention and learning how to use the heavy agency key with a practiced, quick wrist action, one knows that he or she is truly a detention worker when the worker goes around at home locking all the doors while carrying the keys around the house.

Moss

One week the focus was not on the residents in detention, but on the mothers of the residents in detention. Two of my residents found out that their mothers were arrested during that week. Both boys cried out of frustration, out of embarrassment and out of the desperation that in their young lives, more could happen to them in addition to their being in jail.

'I told her,' one of them said. 'I told her this was going to happen. I told her to stop,' he said while he cried. 'I kept telling her. Now, my little brother and sister are in the custody of my grandmother.'

I asked him, 'How many times did she tell you to stop doing what you were doing and how many times didn't you listen to her? You needed to learn your way, the hard way. Sometimes, adults also need to learn the hard way. You didn't listen to her and she didn't listen to you. Sometimes, it takes a few times, a few hard lessons for us to learn.'

'That's true,' he said. Maybe it put things in more of an understandable perspective for him, a shift in perception.

The other one also cried, but his were tears of anger; he was angry at his mom, at his life, at his inability to do anything from inside the walls. His mother was in the same situation in which he found himself.

The aim is to let them feel the feelings, the heat of their tears on their cheeks, the frustration of not being able to take care of family business;

to let them feel the pressures of their own situation and the desperate vows never to get in trouble again. Better to feel it now while they are still young and are in juvenile detention.

How many times does one encounter a solid wall that will absorb the painful blows of desperation, the hot tears of utter dismay, the aching frustration of feeling useless and lost, floundering amid the rules and regulations of detention. Detention is a solid wall that secretly has soft moss clinging to it, which is fertilized by the years of experience of those who create it day by day and continue to build it, mend it, mortar and sandblast it. The solid wall of detention is tempered by those who work within the walls. They are the moss, as soft as velvet, but tenured and strong, caring and experienced. It is said that moss only grows on the North side of a tree, but I tend to disagree, after watching the clinging, tenacious staff who are all over these residents every day while they are in detention.

Spoiled Baby

Detention can bring forth a dichotomy, a double life; one life being the street life, dodging the bullets, the clothes, the talk, the walk.... the life that brings these residents into detention, into one of the more complicated systems in New York City. The other side of the dichotomy is that the residents come from caring families who cannot fathom why their child is drawn like a magnet to the streets and friends.

When a resident comes into detention and meets who will be his caretakers for the duration of his stay, he is forced to accept and deal with them. He is exposed to a great variety of personalities among the staff, but we all know that the residents will do just about anything to get their way. They only know one way...their way. At times, they are spoiled at home and expect the same privileges and conditions in detention, and they are in for a wrenching surprise. The resident is now one among many others and he will receive no special privileges. His pouting will not work. His posturing will not work. His anger will not work. His intimidation and disrespect of the rules and regulations and of others will no longer work in his favor. He wants what he wants. He will keep trying his old methods, the only way he knows to get what he wants, and he will keep running into a wall of rules and staff who will keep reminding him that his old ways will no longer work for him. A scary business for him.

I am reminded of a fifteen-year old resident whose appearance was that of a twenty-five year old. He was husky, strong, street-wise and did not hesitate to think before he began to act out: fighting, cursing and provoking others to become involved in his negative behavior. That was his pattern in the dorm, but on a one-to-one basis, he was respectful and quiet-spoken. He could listen to my advice and counseling, but one can feel when such advice is not really being absorbed and digested and remembered to be used as a future reference, because he kept acting out again when he was in the group. Although he could not seem to listen to my advice, he did seem to form somewhat of a trust in me. I was there if he needed a phone call, envelopes, paper, a pencil, a question answered.

One day, he began to talk. He had a court appearance coming up and he wanted his mother to bring him a particular set of clothing that he wanted to wear before the judge. His mother, on the other hand, wanted him to wear a different outfit. This was a standoff. Both insisted on particular court clothing to be worn at the hearing. My boy said that he knew how to get around this situation to get what he wanted. He said that he always got his way at home. He would call his maternal grandmother who would give the order to his mother to give him what he wanted. If that didn't work, he would call his maternal great grandmother, who would tell his grandmother to tell his mother to give him what he wanted. He smiled as he picked up the phone and said, 'Watch me get what I want. I'm going to snitch on my mother.'

My resident said that his nickname at home was S.B., short for 'Spoiled Baby.' He knew how to put on a pouting and mad face and that would do the trick. It would always work and he would always get his way. He made his call and waited for mountains to be moved for him. I teased him, telling him that one day he would have to give up his baby bottle, and that he was too old to be burped.

As it turned out, he did not win this round in the way he expected. It seems that there was a special reason for his mother wanting him to wear a certain set of clothing to court. She believed that the outfit she had picked out would be impressive and pleasing to the particular judge sitting on her son's case. And she was right. The clothing was pleasing to the judge and after cautioning my boy about his future behavior, the judge reduced his time by six months.

The pattern of baby bottles, pacifiers, burping and pouting was interrupted with a reduced sentenced by a smart mother. My resident was trying to move mountains, with the hope of manipulating his way around her, not realizing that his mother was looking out for her son's best interest.

A Thousand Stars

Occasionally, we have an Asian resident in detention. They, like most of the other residents, may have been in the wrong place at the wrong time, they may have been involved in street activities or illegalities or not, or they may just have become involved in a situation which evolved before they had time to think or back out. In any event, this is the situation with most of the residents.

We have Family Days, which are organized occasions, during which the families of the residents come to visit them in the facility, usually in the large yard or in the gym during inclement weather. The families used to be able to bring in home cooked meals and the aromas from the dishes wafting in the warm summer breeze were wonderful. If I reminisce, I can still detect a hint in the air of the delicious rice and beans, pastilles, pernil, curried chicken, ox tails and home-made cakes, pies and other desserts. All this was replaced by barbecued franks, hamburgers, chicken, salad, punch and icies for dessert when new rules came down from Administration, restricting any more food from being brought into the facility. The popcorn and cotton candy machines, however, were not put out of service with the new regulations, and they continued to be operated by the residents. The residents continued to be considerate waiters for the families and staff and there has never been an incident during a Family Day.

In addition to the Family Days, we have special visits for families, which are arranged when a resident shows consistently good behavior. Again, the family was permitted to bring in home-cooked dishes, and it was especially meaningful when the visit was planned around a resident's birthday. We sometimes stretched the occasions to include a sibling's birthday or a mother or father's birthday, just so we could sample the savory home-cooked dishes. The parent who cooked the meal generally included extra food for some of the staff who worked with the resident.

One of my Asian residents had his special visit and his mother brought in their special meal and dumplings, including an extra portion for me. It was delicious. On another occasion, some of the staff took a few of the residents, including my boy, to the Elite Lounge, which is equipped with all of the necessary kitchen utensils and necessities, and my resident showed off his cooking talents. He even wrote up his own shopping list, which was filled by the Dietary Staff. If the ingredients were not available in the kitchen, staff bought the requested items.

The same resident invited his parents to one of our Family Days. His parents spoke very little English, having come to the U.S. on the run from the Cambodian tragedy. They had escaped from the horrors of their country, went into other Asian countries and eventually made their way to freedom. My resident's father spoke more English than his mother, but even with their limited English, it was evident that they had not yet, and may never, recover from the tragedies experienced at the hand of the dictator. His mother cried with the memories, the horror etched in her expressions, the lines in her face valleys for the tears that continued to flow even after so many years.

Another of my Asian residents also cooked and was also always involved in the cooking sessions in the Elite Lounge when it was made available. He received mail from family and friends, which were opened but not read per procedure, in order to check for contraband or other unwanted items. His letters were folded up in intricate Origami shapes, holding messages only he would know. My boy was a student of Origami himself and he began to create intricate paper foldings that included animals, people, picture frames, baskets, fish, sharks, birds, crabs, seahorses and stars. He occupied his free time creating these forms and staff brought him origami books and special paper for his hobby. He created a meditative atmosphere for himself in a situation in which one can feel lost and alone.

One of his creations was a tiny paper star, made from a long strip of Origami paper. It took him about three minutes or less to make a star and he showed me a large manila envelope filled with so many different colored stars. It was a fascinating sight. He said that he was making one thousand stars and was planning to send them to his girlfriend so that each day she could take one out and put it in a basket, thereby counting the days until he came home, by the stars. We counted his envelope full of stars and we counted 863. He made the rest of the stars while sitting in the day room of his dormitory, during quiet hour, while in his room, or watching TV.

My resident created his own world, and made a thousand stars.

Counseling

In juvenile detention, the catch work, the key work, the 'raison d'etre,' is 'counseling.' In every Tasks and Standards document for those staff members who are in titles indicating that they will be working directly with the residents, the word 'counseling' is mentioned.

Our residents generally come directly off the hot streets of New York City, and packed in their mental and emotional knapsacks are street jargon, street morays and street expectations. It is our job in this facility to wean our children away from the hot skittle which is burning over the open fire of the streets and to pour in the hopeful essences of change. We have several systems in place in detention in the hope of teaching our residents that the stove is hot. In place is a behavior modification system, which rewards and chastises the residents based on their behavior of abiding by the rules and regulations and showing attempts at a productive, positive attitude. We also have positive role models in the form of staff, and we offer programs and rap sessions. All of these attempts at change have within their fabric, the basic tool of 'counseling.'

On every occasion that permits, staff seizes the opportunity to counsel, in whatever area of the building, during whatever program is going on, in the dining room, in rap sessions or in quiet time on the dormitory. We have specialists, such as the staff of our Mental Health Unit, or our School Psychologist, but they often have long lists of children waiting to be seen. The remainder of the staff working directly with the residents is available at all times, at all hours of the day and night to counsel and teach.

One of my boys emanated from a very difficult family situation. The mother and son relationship for which he secretly longed was not forthcoming for him at this stage in his life. He had re-established a relationship with his mother after some years, but it was still fragile and needed time to flourish. He was sent to live with his grandmother, along with his aunt and her children. It was a busy household, not keen on offering him the attention and nourishment he needed; there was free-flowing alcohol in the home, a non-regard for money in terms of letting it go too easily in gambling, and my boy was pushed to the side, to do the best he could.

He was a pleasant kid, a friendly being who began to trust me after a few months. I asked him a question about his mother and he said that when I had some time, he would tell me about his family because he trusted me. That day came unannounced after he spoke to his family on the phone. The phone conversation was stressful for him and he did not receive the support from his family that he was craving, which opened up the door for me to peek in and start to talk to him and to counsel him. Surprisingly, he did not speak in a selfish, childish manner, but rather said that he was feeling so badly that he could not do anything to help his family, to try to stop the flow of alcohol, which he had tried to do by pouring it down the drain. He had an overwhelming guilty conscience, but did not know why, and only felt its paralyzing weight. Why was his family so alienating, he wondered; why were they unable to give him his teenage years; why was his relationship with his mother so difficult and late in developing. He realized that during these years, he would be making normal demands on her that he knew she was not yet ready to handle. This was a bright kid in front of me.

I began to talk to him from the depth of my own experiences, from life, from lifting him up, from wanting to present him with positive choices, from using myself as the best tool I had at my disposal, as I had been taught. I talked and scrutinized his expression along the way, watching his eyes, measuring the inches of his comprehension with visual clues, to see if I was making any impact, inroads. I also asked if what I was saying made any sense to him and skipped over some material, telling him that he already knew all that since he was smart and that he did not need lecturing. His changing, thoughtful expression told me that I was making contact with some of his inner thoughts. For the 'denouement,' I made a statement that emerged from my own experience, and he finally said, 'I'm glad you broke that down for me.' He smiled with a recognition of something vital and rich within him as he continued to climb out of the guilt-laden valley into which he had wandered.

I received positive feedback from him when he shook my hand, said he would talk to me again, when he told his mother that I was 'looking out for him' and called me his friend, but these were by-products, although gladly accepted and appreciated. The essence of the interaction was knowing that my boy could maybe shrug off some old, dusty emotions of guilt and depression and separate himself from those aspects of his family that were not helping him grow. After all, he was not responsible for other people's lives, for their habits, for their not being able to give to him. These things were not his fault. I told him that the only things he was responsible for were: whatever he allegedly did in the street and only he knew that truth; getting his education; separating himself from negative people; choosing to interact with those who would be positive for him; and for living his life.

I gave my boy a potholder, so that even if he wanted to touch the hot stove again, out of habit or curiosity, maybe he would have a little more protection this time, a little more insight so that he would not get scalded. I told him that if he needed to hear all of our conversation again, I would be glad to talk to him, to 'counsel' him, and to give him as many potholders and oven mitts as he needed.

Credit Where Credit is Due

I have to give them credit for trying. After the meals are served, the chores are done, the school day is over, the phone calls are made, the rap sessions are finished....what is left for a resident in detention but time on his hands? I watch them sometimes in the yard. Some play chess, some play basketball or softball, some talk to staff, some play handball, and some just sit and think: how to get over. 'How can I get what I want even though it's contraband or against the rules?'

One of the vital avenues in detention is, of course, connection to family. This is arranged through phone calls or via visiting. Visiting has been, and will probably always be, an area of detention that is pulsing with possibilities or 'getting over.' Very often, names will be given by a parent for the visiting list that are not appropriate or permitted, such as a girlfriend's name being given in the guise of being a sister. I have always been peeved by this practice, since it sets a bad example for the resident, and the resident is in detention to learn, not to continue his old ways.

I had a resident who received regular visits from his mother and 'sister.' All procedures were followed. The sister was of the proper age; her name, address and birthdate were verified by my resident's mother and the young lady had proper identification. What could be wrong with this picture? But there was something wrong in how my resident related to his 'sister' in the visiting area. Brothers and sisters didn't act that way towards each other. However, they quickly got wise to those watching them and they cooled their act. The Supervisor, who was experienced in these things, knew they were not siblings, but could not prove otherwise right away. She kept a vigil over the visiting area for over a year. She was persistent in her hunch that these two just did not fit the picture. She shared her belief with the Director, who began to do some legwork outside of the agency. He went to the 'sister's' place of employment, which turned out to be her place of unemployment, since she was not known to them, had never been known to them and had never worked there. Her I.D. was fake, her story was fake and the resident's mother's verification that this was her daughter was fake. The young lady was my resident's girlfriend all along. Not to condone this weaving of untruths, but I have to give them credit for trying. This sham lasted longer than any other in my experience. I also have to give the Supervisor a lot of credit for her tenacity in following through with her long-term hunch and I told her so.

I was in the yard one time looking for one of my residents. Another resident came over to me and began to talk about a visitor, his brother, he wanted to add to the visiting list. He had just seen his Case Manager, who had spoken to his mother and the mother began to give the name and birthdate of a cousin. A cousin? Everyone knows that cousins cannot visit in juvenile detention. The resident had been on the phone with his mother, upset that she was saying cousin instead of brother and he was relating this story to me…

'Can you do something to get my cousin on the list?' he asked me. I laughed and said, 'You blew it. You just said your cousin. Cousins don't visit here.'

'Oh, no!' he said, 'I meant to say my brother. I'm just upset at my mother for getting this all mixed up.' I said,' I understand that you're upset, but it's too late. That's really your cousin, right?'

'No' he insisted, 'It's my cous….I mean my brother.'

I laughed again.

He went on, 'No, it's my c…my brother.' Even he had to laugh this time.

'Can you tell the Supervisor that I want to see her so that I can explain this whole thing?' he asked. 'That's no problem,' I told him. 'She's out for a few days, but when she comes back, I'll tell her that you want to talk to her so that you can get your cous….I mean your brother on the visiting list.'

We looked at each other and laughed and shook hands.

The interaction was a whole lot of fun. That was either his brother or cousin or maybe even a friend. His story got mixed up and he is mad at his mother for not handling her end of it. But, I have to give him credit for trying…for standing out there next to the radio in the yard, while everyone else was playing basketball, handball, playing chess, cards, talking or just listening to the music…for standing there, using his recreation time to think of a way to get over.

Why Do Children Fight?

Those of us who work with children in detention often become friendly with many of them. We are with them all hours of the day, and practically live with them. The Juvenile Counselors are with them on the dormitories twenty-four hours a day in three shifts, and they become family. At one time or another, family members disagree, argue, do not get along or fight. When twenty-four residents live together in a dormitory area, especially teen-age boys, who are raring and ready for anything that comes their way, it is almost normal for occasional fights and flare-ups to erupt. They happen so fast, in a flash, often without warning. If there is a lot of verbiage, gesturing and challenging talk and stances, we know and they know that they will most likely not take it to the next physical level. They are really giving the staff fair warning to come and break up the dissention and situation before it escalates. While they give the impression that there will be no holding back, they never get to throw a punch. When they are really going to fight, they just start to fight in a flash, in the snap of a finger, without warning to staff to 'come and hold me back.'

There are areas of detention in which the residents are told that fighting is a 'no-no.' One such 'out of bounds' area is the dining room, where there are hard, plastic trays that can be used as battering rams or flying missiles, and where there are too many residents in one large area at a time during meals. In fact, after one such riot, dormitories were fed one or two at a time instead of an entire unit, which included four dormitories of ninety-six children. The turning point occurred as a result of such a melee during which two residents jumped on one of the tables, and standing back to back, they gestured and kicked as if they were making a ninja movie.

Holidays are a time of stress for children in detention, as is understandable. Although they are accused of crimes, with the term 'alleged' tacked next to their charge, they are still children. They are away from their families, they are homesick and uncomfortable, they cry, and at times, they act out. I remember one Christmas when the residents decorated the dormitory as if it were home…lights strung around the day room, glittering Christmas wrapping paper covering the walls and bulletin boards, foils of all the Christmas colors wrapped around the pillars, music and a beautiful artificial tree covered with tinsel, glistening balls and wrapped (empty) boxes underneath. I helped the residents paint a mural of reindeer and Santa and the whole effect was impressive. In fact, our dorm won the prize for the best decorated hall.

What started it, we never found out. It started in a flash, not a 'hold me back' fight. With the energy and force of a rising tidal wave, everyone erupted at once. The staff of three had no chance of stopping the momentum. I was in the area and was fortunately close to the rear of the dayroom in the dormitory. Separating the dayroom from the long corridor of rooms was a Plexiglas partition and a locked door. As I unlocked the door to step out of the line of fire of flying objects, I watched the beautiful Christmas tree fly from one side of the dorm to the other. If it were not such a serious breach of every rule of detention, I would have said that the residents were having a good time. At least, it relieved some of their holiday stress.

I pushed the panic button on the wall because things were really getting out of control. I did manage to bring one of the boys with me behind the partition, so at least he was out of harm's way and he would be prevented from being punished for any involvement in the melee. Security came running. Order was restored. Everyone was placed in his room and counseling sessions began. Incident reports flowed and became part of the daily facility package of reports that is sent downtown to the Commissioner's office.

There had been a tornado in the dormitory, but the residents were not transported to make-believe land. After the riot, they were still in detention. They could not click their heels to create another reality; they had to take the consequences and responsibility for the colorful Christmas trimmings that were flying around the day room.

After the tinsel stopped shimmering, after the Christmas balls came to a halt against the walls and furniture, after the Christmas lights stopped flickering and the empty wrapped gift boxes were gathered, after the residents served their punishment, it was back to business as usual in detention.

A Serious Business

There are many facets of detention, many of which are structured and predictable and the staff makes every attempt to maintain this structure among both the residents and co-workers. It is somewhat comforting to be able to fit the pieces of the detention puzzle into their respective, receptive spots so that one's day can go as planned. However, as in any large organization, and especially when people, and children in particular, are the main focus, the best laid plans…..

One of the more important topics of counseling residents focuses on respect for others. Without respect in this facility, a resident is often fighting against a strong, upstream current, against rocky rapids on which he can be bruised and battered, emotionally and otherwise. Counseling, rap sessions and daily experiences are all grasped and turned into teaching residents about respect for others. That and diligent and constant supervision and observation generally maintain a high level of good behavior among the residents.

However, there are times when things happen so quickly that there is not enough time for staff to intervene and stop a fight. There are other times, and the residents know just when these times and places are, which offer an optimum opportunity to 'take care of business.' One of these times and places is in the 'bull pen' in the court building, which is an area for residents who are waiting to be brought before their judges to attend their hearings. Since the level of supervision is not as vigilant as in the detention facility, things may happen.

This brings to mind a resident of mine who was one of the hundreds of differing personalities brought together in detention for as many different reasons, backgrounds, problems, fear and needs. My resident already had a difficulty family situation and had been living with various relatives while his mother was dealing with her own issues. He was unfortunately in the 'wrong place at the wrong time' as is the situation with many of our youngsters, and received a nasty slash along the side of his face.

This is a resident who had been doing everything requested of him on his dormitory, including chores, helping others, abiding by the rules and regulations, showing respect for others, and maintaining a good humor and positive attitude. However, his internal and bubbling anger at what had happened to him 'in the street' and which had not been dealt with on a verbal and emotional level, finally found its release and erupted in the bull pen when he hit another resident with all of the force and ferocity that had been previously aimed at him. It was a serious injury and the boy who had been hit was having double, unfocused vision and was hemorrhaging behind his eye.

My boy, who was usually so quiet and unassuming, was in big trouble. He had another assault charge looming over him with the possibility of more time and transfer to an adult prison. Counseling started, a referral to our Mental Health Unit was written, restriction had started the minute he returned from court and the staff was surprised at this kind of incident occurring, especially with this particular resident. This was a serious situation. Administration was informed and I informed the boy's family that he was in trouble and on restriction. There were vital ramifications to be considered: the other boy's eyesight was at stake and more years of incarceration for my resident would be considered. If he did not deal with this well of anger now, he was likely to do this again and again.

Needless to say, since these are still children, it was felt that they still have a chance. The other resident's eye had a good chance of healing since he was in good health and my resident's life had a good chance of healing since he was still open to change. We were dealing here with some core aspects of life: anger, revenge, change, caring, teaching and hope.

Detention is a serious business.

Children of Children

When a resident comes into detention, if he is new to the system, he may feel emotionally assaulted by a barrage of questions. Along with an admission physical, presentations by the clergy, the ombudsperson and staff who will be working with him in the dormitory, he is subject to an Intake Interview from a Case Manager. Among questions about his education, health, court status, hobbies and likes and dislikes, he is asked questions about his family situation and whether or not he has any children of his own.

Many of our residents started a family early in life. I have found that contrary to the common belief, the majority of those who have children, feel a caring and natural bonding with their babies. They realize that they are too young, have not yet begun to form their own lives, cannot support the child or the young mother and have added a new responsibility on their own mothers who generally help care for the child. Sometimes, the young mother and baby come to live in the resident's home so that the child can be reared in a family setting in which the young father will eventually be a vital part of the child's life.

The resident who has a child can hardly wait to become eligible for a special visit, which is attained with good behavior on the Behavior Modification System. At that time, he can see his child. I am always interested to observe the interaction, bonding and relationship that is formed and growing between father and son or daughter. Since the baby is brought in by the resident's mother, she often coaches her son on how to hold or feed the baby. 'Talk to him,' one of my mothers told her son. 'He will learn to know your voice, to know that you are his father.' After giving his baby a bottle and looking at the little one with awe and disbelief that this was his own, a part of him, at the point he feels something warm beginning to pool at the other end of the bottle, is the point at which he hands his offspring back to his mother. Changing diapers begins, and very often a resident, who has had experience with younger brothers and sisters meets the challenge head on.

One of my boys whose girlfriend had given birth to a daughter prior to his coming into detention, had attended the birth as well as birthing classes, and knew the names of all of the methods and procedures that his girlfriend had experienced. This particular resident was in the detention and court system on a misdemeanor charge and was eventually placed by the court in a group home located near his home. After school, he was able to get passes to see his new family and become an integral part of their lives, which was what he craved. He had a very strong incentive to complete his education, get a job and support his family.

There were a few residents in my dorm who were afraid to tell their mothers of a new arrival. The time and place to share this event with their mothers was always their choice, and in all of these situations, they did eventually tell their mothers of their new stature as 'grandmother.'

When the term 'children having children' is voiced, it is generally accepted by most people as a situation that will be fraught with its own difficulties and burdens. It is a term, however, that is heard and accepted at a surface or more shallow level than the reality it represents. The reality forms when a youth in detention sees and holds his one-year old son or daughter and forges that bond with his child that will last a lifetime. At that moment, he may begin his life over. At that moment, we have the hope of helping him do just that.

Growing Up

I believe that the longer a youth remains in detention, the better off he is. This belief has been reinforced over and over again during the years that I have been working in the system, and the only 'codicil' that I would add to that firm belief is that very often, a youth does not remain long enough and is often released too soon.

It takes a number of years for a child to form into the youngster he is and it takes a long time to undo many of the negative scales under which he has hidden himself. If he remains with us long enough, the inevitable will almost certainly occur. The resident will begin to shed his former years of the streets and negative peer pressure and will slowly begin to stretch his limbs and his mind, sloughing off the dried scales of his past.

I knew of a resident in detention for over a year. He was not on my caseload, but I would see him so often around the building or in his dormitory that we would acknowledge each other. If his own worker was out or on vacation, I would deliver mail to him and others in his group. This was his fifth admission to detention, hence the moniker 'revolving door.' I saw his continuous admissions as an unknowing attempt on his part to 'do it until he got it right;' to come into a structured environment where he knew he would not be able to do as he wanted; to learn how to control himself; to handle himself with others; to test the walls and boundaries of his surroundings in order to find out where his own walls and boundaries began and ended.

I finally got him. He was assigned to me when he was transferred and upgraded into a more mature, older group, since that is the age group with whom I worked. He was polite and respectful, but reserved and reticent to share and he remained as such for a long time. He got into mischief and fights, but regrouped and recouped and continued to grow within. He continued his upward bound ascent and graduated into becoming a closet boy, which carries a certain amount of trust, responsibility and respect among his peers and staff.

He began to trust, as the soiled and cracked scales began to peel back, as he began to emerge and stretch and reach out for advice from those who knew more than he did. He had needed time for those scales to restrict his growth, for him to feel uncomfortable enough to allow them to release and to allow new growth and maturity to emerge.

He asked to speak to me one day, and asked if I would give him some advice about his girlfriend from a woman's point of view. This was a big step, an important gift, since he was willing to change his former way of handling his emotions and thoughts, which was more often than not in a physical, impulsive manner. He was willing to try a new way, confronting his emotions, validating them with someone else and dealing with them in a calmer, more acceptable way. I offered the best advice I could and he said that he would let me know the outcome of his venture. I never did learn of the results since he left the facility and moved elsewhere to complete his time.

I thought about him later and wished he could have stayed even longer with us in detention. His staff knew that he was already on his way to becoming a mature young man, but he had to move on, hopefully taking with him some of what we had tried to instill in him. We wanted him to be another of our success stories.

Another of our residents was with us for over two years on a serious charge. When he was admitted to the facility, he was a little wild and got into fights and arguments with other residents and staff had to keep a close eye on him. It took him time, but he began to calm down and became more aware of the rules and expectations of him. He attended our school regularly with no more fighting and began to gain the respect of his staff who watched him slowly change and mature. His family continued to visit and support him and slowly, over the years he was with us, he became a model resident known and liked throughout the facility.

He took his Regents and passed them all and did so well in our school, that he graduated with a Regents Endowed High School Diploma. He continued to keep in touch with us and we assisted him in gathering information and paperwork; he got his State I.D. and registered for college.

Another success story!

I have to include here that another of our residents who started to come to our facility at age eleven, came and went, in an out of our facility throughout the years, amassing a total of nine admissions into and out of detention. He was always a difficult resident, fought and hit other residents without apparent reason and had a hard time listening to and abiding by the regulations and directives of his staff. We watched him grow up, but he only seemed to grow up physically; he did not mature nor was he able to utilize the counseling that was offered to him. He had become slightly more aware of acceptable social expectations over the years, but on the whole, he remained a difficult resident until he left at age seventeen. Maybe his next placement or home experience will force him or help him to finally grow up.

A Puzzlement

There are times in detention when things seem incongruous; they don't fit together as if one could say, 'something is wrong with this picture.' There are times when we see a resident in detention who has hardworking parents and brothers and sisters who are doing well and who may be in college. If anyone were to observe that resident, watching his habits, his interactions with his peers, with adults, one might say that he could be headed toward college on a scholarship.

One such resident is brought to mind. He was a tall, outgoing youth who had a presence of leadership about him. Others in his dormitory looked up to him, not only because he was 6'7" and 185 pounds at 15-years old, but because he was respected and liked by the other residents. He had a comradery with many staff members because he was mature and adult-like, although still a child in many ways. He had a dream of becoming a pro-basketball player and told me that many of the best high schools were scouting him. His basketball coach still maintained contact with his mother and the coach continued to track the whereabouts of his future star.

This was a puzzlement, this incongruous picture before me, and we began to talk. He said that his older sister and older brother were both in college and his parents were both working. He had everything he needed at home. He did not need any money since he received an adequate allowance; he had enough clothes and sneakers to wear to school to give the desired impression to the girls and to his friends; he knew that he had a promising future because he was being pursued by prestigious high schools. The pieces of the puzzle were not fitting. I tried to rearrange the pieces and press them into their spaces, but to no avail. I could not formulate a rationale for this resident being in the predicament in which he found himself.

I asked him how he got into this mess, into the system, into detention. The answer he offered was telling and showed something of our society today. He said that he had joined in with a group, knew that a robbery was going to occur and 'just wanted to see what it was like.' This was an honest statement from a 15-year old who was mature beyond his years in many aspects of his life, but did not yet have a solid, molded measure of judgment to stop him from 'just wanting to see.'

He looked back on his actions, on himself involved in something negative, out of character, and shook his head, trying to help those pieces of his life float down and settle around him again. He was the little figure in the glass ball, the bits of his life swirling in slow motion around him, trying to reform and recreate his life.

As Long As It's Outside

Although juvenile detention offers a great deal to the children who are living within its walls, the one thing that is unavailable to them is freedom. They are told when to line up, when to sit down, when to have quiet hour, when to go to school, when to eat, when to shower, when to go to sleep and they have to ask permission if they want to get up to drink water or use the bathroom. They were not thinking about the adage that most of us know, of not knowing the real value of something until it is gone.

One of my residents who was already sixteen years old and a very mature and personable youth, was in my office, on the phone with his cousin. He was with us for about a year and a half and had developed good social skills as well as insight into his own thoughts and behavior. His phone conversations were generally ones that were infused with concern for his family, future plans, visiting and other vital aspects of his life. His phone conversation on that particular day with his cousin caused me to look up at him. He was talking about petty things, asking silly kinds of questions and continued to prompt this kind of conversation flow.

He asked his cousin, 'You went to the store? What did you buy? Juice? What kind? Orange? Why not grape? Did you drink it there or take it home? Did you go straight home or walk around? What else did you do? What else did you buy?'

He laughed at my questioning expression which prompted him to explain, 'I never get tired of hearing a conversation and will ask anything just to keep a conversation going. I never get tired of hearing a conversation as long as it's outside.'

He reminded me of that cartoon of a cartoon character who is running and comes to the edge of a cliff, running right off the cliff, and continuing to remain in mid air as long as he thinks he is still running on solid ground. As soon as he looks down at reality, his descent begins. My boy had been with us for a long time and knew that he was benefiting and growing every day, but that longing for family and freedom is undeniably ingrained in us all. He was finding creative ways in the form of orange and grape juice, to keep himself afloat, in mid air without looking down, during the remainder of his time until he returned home.

Conversations

Not that I'm being nosey, but we do have to monitor the conversations of our residents. At times, they ask to make a private call, but this is not permitted, since the resident and his phone calls have to be monitored at all times. He is not left alone at any time since we know how easily they can get into 'mischief.' Much of the time, when they are on the phone, we half listen to the conversation, but we perk up when he begins to talk in a low tone to the other party, or we hear him planning something that he is not supposed to be planning. Sometimes, he includes us in his conversation with facial expressions aimed at the other party and we think, 'If only the person on the other end of the line could see him.' Sometimes the conversations are poignant and sweet.

'Yes, mommy,' said one resident, 'I love you too. I can't wait to come home. Is anyone using my room? Is anyone wearing my clothes? I go to court tomorrow and I hope they let me go. If they let me go, I'm going to do a backflip...but I don't know how to do a backflip.'

Or...'You got the job, mommy?' said another resident. 'I'm so happy for you!'

Or...'No, mom, I don't want you to come to visit me at night. I'll worry about you getting home.'

Or...'I just wanted to check on the family,' from a homesick resident. 'How's everyone doing? What are you cooking? I don't care when you come to see me, just as long as you visit me.'

Or...'I understand you have the other kids to look after,' from a resident who was growing up before my eyes. 'You don't have to visit me today...take care of them so they don't end up like me. I should have listened to you.'

Not all conversations are poignant and sweet, however. There is often animosity between mother and son or between father and son and this is a challenge for the staff. This is a situation that generally begins long before our resident comes into the system. It is a situation that we try to work with, rectify and rejuvenate, but it is not easy. The relationship between mother and son is important and one that will determine a youth's future relationships with women, friends and many others who will pass through his life. We have experienced residents who will not talk to their mothers and will not go into the visiting area if she comes to visit. In this situation, staff members who have formed a relationship with the resident try to talk to him into relenting, to start to deal with this vital aspect of his young life. If he refuses to see her, the counseling will not stop, and in fact will continue until the youth agrees either out of frustration at all of the attempts at counseling him, or just to get staff to leave him alone.

In every situation I know of, in which a resident refused to see his mother, that situation was reversed in time, to the credit of staff, and a new, tenuous attempt at reconciliation was generated. During those new, fragile relationships, I used to observe both mother and son being very conscious of their dialogue, and both tried not to repeat old and warn out diatribes that they employed in the past. It was a struggle since both wanted to continue to express anger, tears and hurt out of habit and perhaps not knowing what else to do, but both also wanted to reconnect a relationship that they both vitally needed.

'OK, mommy, I love you mommy.'

Feedback

We usually do not know what happens to our residents when they leave us. If they are sentenced, we do know that they will be going to one of a number of juvenile facilities all over the state, and occasionally, but not usually, to a specialized facility out of state, per the Interstate Compact procedures. If sentenced, they will remain under the umbrella of the large agency that handles, places and plans for all of those children the Courts have deemed worthy of doing time, to give back for what they were found to have taken.

But what happens when the residents have completed their time and have returned home under the supervision of an Aftercare Worker, who looks after them in the community? What happens when they gingerly put their hand out from under the umbrella to see if it is drizzling, raining, sleeting…to see what the world has waiting for them? They have been in a secured place, away from those temptations that induced and seduced them in the first place. They have hopefully learned a new way of handling themselves, based on counseling, the role model of their staff, and sometimes, just growing up. They have calmed down, mellowed, matured with us and we have tried to give them as many tools as we can to help them when they are finally released home.

Sometimes the staff talks about some of the residents: how he was when he was in detention; how many times it took for him to be on restriction to finally learn that what he was doing was not acceptable; how often he got into arguments or fights; how much counseling we all did with him; how his mother had thrown up her hands with frustration and sadness that she could not seem to do anything to help her son.

We sometimes see our boys outside in the community and most of the feedback is that they are doing fine, that they are going to school, that they thank us for what we tried to do to help them. Recently, a man was behind me in line in a community store, with a nine or ten year old with him. He smiled and said, 'Hi, how're you doing? Do you remember me?' I looked at him and thought that he looked a little familiar. He told me his name and said that he was in our facility almost fifteen years ago. He looked well, and looked as if he was doing well; I told him so, he said he was doing fine and introduced his son.

I then asked the pressing question…'Did we help you while you were in our facility?' I watched his face as he suddenly became the fifteen-year old again, traveling back in time to his experience in juvenile detention…he slowly and solemnly shook his head yes; his past experience compacted into seconds of remembrance. He then came back to the present…..another success story!

But, too often, we hear that one of our former residents was shot, wounded or killed. This is very sad and a waste of a young life who could not or would not take what we were practically forcing on him, almost spoon feeding him about the need for him to change his life.

And, very often we hear from them by mail:

'To Mr./Ms.….,

It's me, Sammy. I'm doing fine out here. You will always be the greatest staff / teacher / Security / Caseworker. I love you and I thank you for what you did for me.'

What can I say? It's the best!

A Test

The weaknesses of some are the strengths of others; one man's meat is another man's poison; where we lack in some areas, other fill in those spaces.....Those residents who are fourteen and fifteen-years old are very often old beyond their years. They have a different focus in life from others in the same age group who are in different life situations and circumstances. They are already involved in relationships and many have children of their own. They are often going through the emotional turmoil that young adults in their twenties are often just beginning.

One of my fifteen-year old residents had a six-month old daughter who was being cared for by the baby's mother. He could not physically care for the baby, he felt for her, felt responsibility for her, for her future, and he was showing concern beyond his years, although he himself was a child in many ways.

He used to talk back to staff and got into fights without thinking for a split second about what he was doing. I came to work one morning and found out why they call a black eye a 'shiner.' My boy had gotten into a fight the evening before and wouldn't even try to say that he had won that one. The evidence was too strong against him. The whole eye, socket and all, spreading out to his temple, was shining black and blue and I almost had to shield my eyes from the reflection of the light. Usually, residents enjoy extra attention, but not this time. My resident walked around the building somewhat embarrassed. He couldn't hide the shining fact that he had lost a fight.

After the incident, after the doctors determined that his retina and sight were not damaged, and after several weeks, as the shiner faded to a light purple and blue, my boy began to mellow.

He began to talk. The focus of his conversation was on his life, his future, trying to push away the weeds of the natural confusion of his age, to make space for himself to slip through, to try to begin to understand the meaning of everything he was going through and everything he was putting everyone else through. But, what he felt most for, the thing that warmed his heart, was a girl. She was not his baby's mother; this was someone else, someone he liked.

When he began to talk to her on the phone, he began to woo her, laying it on thick, not to show off, but because he really liked her and wanted to impress her. He began to ask her questions as if he were giving her an exam, hoping that she would pass his test. He gave her scenarios to think about. One involved her methods of handling a situation involving an imaginary little girl. Another concerned balancing funds, saving money and bank accounts. He was covering all of his bases. After he completed his conversation with her, he seemed satisfied that she had passed.

My boy had so many things going on in his life: his court situation, the lack of contact with his mother for several years, the possibility of doing time upstate away from his family and daughter. With so many other things on his mind, at this time in his life when he was under so many varied pressures, it is hard to understand that his focus was on looking for a girlfriend.

My resident was a child in many ways and he began to wear his shiner proudly since he could not hide it. He used to act like a spark, fighting and arguing without thinking, causing disruption in the group and he was a handful for the staff who worked with him. But, in other ways, he was far ahead of many others older than he who were still trying to find themselves. My boy's life had already found him and he was trying to work it out the best way he knew how.

We All Cry

Along with my pad, pen and a list of residents on my caseload, there were three more essential items that I carried around with me when I made my rounds in the facility. I am a notary, and provided this service for the facility. The first two essential items were my notary stamp along with the notary ledger book, which recorded all of my notarizations. Almost every day, someone on the job needed something to be notarized. Since it was difficult for staff to leave their posts, not being able to leave the residents unsupervised, I made 'house calls,' on the dorms, carrying my notary equipment. The in-house service was mobile.

The other item I carried around was tissues. New residents who come into detention are very often confused, afraid and homesick. The sound of a mother's voice is enough to evoke and provoke unbridled tears and a hiccupping, breathless, uncontrolled hyperventilation within a youth. We have all experienced this depth of despair and tears, and although we sympathize and empathize, the first action we must take is to calm the youth, telling him to take a deep breath, to breathe, in order to control his uncontrolled surge of emotion. The tough guy on the street becomes a child again.

One of the new residents I interviewed was experiencing that surge of breathlessness and flow of tears when he spoke to his mother. While he was talking to her, I was trying to calm him down and while he was crying, with the tears streaming down his face, being sopped up by tissue after tissue, he was smiling at me. I thought that maybe he felt appreciative of my attempts to make him feel better, but at the same time, he was sobbing for his mother and for the state in which he found himself. This is the first time I saw two opposite emotions being played out so dramatically at the same time, alternating as if a page were being flipped back and forth to create movement in a drawing or cartoon.

I spoke to his mother as well, and had to assure her that her son was in good hands and that he was only afraid because this was a new experience for him. If I had another package of tissues with me, I would have had to offer them to his mother, since she was experiencing her own surge of tears, guilt and a myriad of other maternal emotions.

I had another resident who had been in detention for about a year while his court case was still pending. He made regular phone contacts with his mother and appeared to have close family ties. His mother regularly brought him changes of clothing for his court appearances and his case was finally coming to fruition and disposition. The District Attorney finally made him an offer, a plea bargain, of three to nine years. My boy was shocked. He was fantasizing and hoping for a one to three year offer and he spoke to his mother about the possibility of lower time. His mother was more practical than my resident, and a few years for her son to be off the streets did not phase her at all. In fact, she welcomed the fact that she did not have to cringe whenever the phone rang, or wait for the dreaded knock on her door.

My resident received his weekly phone calls home and started to plead with his mother to do something so that he would not have to do three or more years. He cried and out came the tissues again. His mother could not do anything. He would ask her repeatedly to try to talk to the attorney, to anyone who could help him, but she could do nothing. He was her son and she loved him with all her heart, but she could not do anything anymore. This was out of her hands and her son's future was in the hands of the court system.

My boy finally asked her to 'Habla con tu santo, mommy, please mommy, I love you and I'll never do anything wrong again.' For three or four weeks, he pleaded with his mother to talk to her saint, and she finally did, and she had an answer for her son. Her saint advised him to do the time.

My boy eventually took the plea of three to nine and was sent upstate to do his time. His mother's saint was smart. He didn't want the boy on the streets any more than his mother did. My boy went to school upstate, got his GED, and when he finally came home, he tried to avoid the same friends and influences, dodging bullets, running the streets, stashing weapons, wearing the clothes, taking the pose, talking the prose....that led him into detention in the first place.

Weekends

Think....mellow, relaxed, no stress, chilly and damp outside, but cozy and safe inside, hot and humid outside and cool and comfortable inside...and this is the feeling of weekends in detention. The tone is down, the music is low, and the residents can stay in their pajamas like kids.

After breakfast on Saturday, the group returns to the dormitory and begins chores of cleaning their rooms, scrubbing the furniture, and mopping and waxing the floors and this is termed 'Major Clean-Up.' After the chores are done, the day is pretty much theirs. They can sleep, play chess, play cards, write letters, read or contemplate their lives. There is no school and they may have an assigned recreation period. They may go out to the yard depending on the weather; they may watch a football, basketball or baseball game on TV, depending on the season; they may watch a movie, pop their own popcorn and make their own punch.

Sunday is a day of church services, rest and an extra low tone. The staff is more relaxed with the low tone and it is, on the whole, a time out, a breathing space, a regrouping after a busy week. Although usually always vigilant and alert, the low tone offers staff a more relaxed couple of days.

Is it too easy for the residents? Are we making it too comfortable for them? Not really. They still follow a structured routine and they are not free to move around the building on their own. They have basically forfeited their freedom. They may or may not have experienced structure at home and if not, it can be the start of a good foundation. They came into detention bringing the streets along with them. If they stay with us long enough, they will leave carrying a gift of building blocks that they can form into a new structure for their lives. Even if the blocks are carved with a child's ABC's, our residents have to start somewhere.

Talent

Detention is a pulsating, living community in which a myriad of beings, both residents and staff, thrive. The waves of humanity undulate to an emotional rhythm, based in a root system that is fed by encouragement and hope.

Scattered among the large number of inhabitants of this system are a variety of talented people, residents and staff alike. I have met some of the most talented people, who could have gone on to a professional career in their fields, if they were not already doing so. Singers, including gospel, jazz and modern, a very talented cartoonist, tenor sax player, piano player, athletes, cooks, essayists, artists….and that is just the staff. The residents have proven to show a great deal of potential as well and I have seen dancers, cooks, athletes, bakers, rappers, singers and budding artists and writers among those youths I have known.

One of the highlights of the detention year is a talent / fashion show. These residents have a sense of fashion and put together a musical sensation that rivals any professional show. They strut down the runway, which is really an aisle between rows of chairs, to taped music and show off their outfits with a flair. Following the show is a lively talent show and I wish that scouts could see some of the talent that is presented.

During time in detention, the pressure of the street and peer pressure is lifted from their impressionable shoulders and they have time to stop, evaluate and consider what they would like to begin to place in their futures. They have time to peer within and see what has been inside them all along, waiting to have a chance to become evident. One of my residents began to write poetry that began to tap feelings he had shuttered away for many years. His writing was mature and expressive. He showed great promise, and the staff encouraged him to write more and to consider writing for the residents' newsletter that was being organized.

Another resident was involved in a cooking program with staff. His specialty was brownies that were far better than those purchased in the store. He was beaming after he finished a batch of his tasty, rich brownies, proud to have produced something so good.

Many of the residents have a natural sporting ability and have joined the detention basketball team. We also have flag football teams (tackling might encourage them to vent *too* much of their aggressiveness and assertiveness) as well as handball, volleyball and softball and their talents become evident.

I have told several of my boys that maybe I should get their autographs now because when they become famous, they won't have time and will forget all about us. I am truly glad they came to detention so that some of these natural talents have a chance to bud and produce the nectar of a more hopeful future.

Jumpers, Pleats and Headphones

Remaining in detention for a lengthy period of time has its advantages besides the expected maturing process, polishing social skills and learning how to relate to others without rancor, anger or revenge. If one observes the residents on a dorm, groupings seem to take form naturally, as water seeks its own level. Those who are new to the group watch and learn until it is their time to assume leadership.

The steps leading up to the pinnacle of dorm leadership are replete with adornments and privileges: those who can and cannot listen to stereo music with private headphones; those who can or cannot use the iron to iron their jumpers, their uniforms; and those who can or want to make ironing designs in their jumpers.

Most of us who iron, try to iron out the creases. Those at the top of the leadership ladder in the dormitory deliberately iron pleats, folds and nicknames into the material of their jumpers. They may have ironed pleats from the waist down on one day, or if their mood changes, they may iron pleats into the sleeves only. Spelling out nicknames is more complicated. Of course, bad words are not allowed. It is really very creative.

Many of the residents have a great deal of creativity and potential. During the period of time in which they have no choice but to be with us, after they settle in, they come to realize that they do not have to constantly look over their shoulders, 'watch their back,' or live in fear. It is then that the dormant, latent creative processes begin to awaken.

The resident's own inner growth and bubbling creative juices may even take him or her by surprise. One creative door opens the next one and he starts a process of knowing himself and his value.

I had a resident on my dorm who loved to color. I provided him with pages from a coloring book and colored pencils and he was quite creative in his shading and adding his own touches 'outside the lines.' A project was being organized in the facility in which some of the interested residents would be participating in creating a mural on a large wall. My resident was very interested and his name was offered as a willing participant. As the mural took form, his imagination bloomed and he was an integral part of the designing and painting project. From a coloring book to a wall mural. What potential that offered for him!

This process takes time, but it is time well spent; time invested in the futures of children. There is really no other choice.

A Shuttle

When a shuttle is launched into the endless sky after years of perfecting the engines, tweeking the systems, every wire and every computer chip, the missile is turned to the heavens, headed towards its destination. Along the way, it sloughs off its rockets and its booster rockets, leaving the small, perfected shuttle to make its way, filled with planning and programming, to find its way in the vastness of space, to arrive at its destination with future hope.

The staff in detention are the booster rockets, fired up with the goal of guiding our residents, teaching them about a different universe, re-programming and re-wiring them, giving them the best opportunity for an optimum launch into life.

It is sometimes a tedious, difficult and exhausting challenge, but it is one that is done with care and concern, at full throttle. The forces of the streets, of former mores, work to pull the resident out of orbit, precariously aiming him back to his old life. The staff uses the tools of counseling, example, and any other positive means to keep the shuttle focused and on course.

We know that the residents in detention are a segment of society that cannot be ignored and disowned. They are a part of us all. Since they are young, they still have the potential to make a maiden voyage into their lives, to reach out and embrace their own destinations, their own futures.

We also know that the children are our future and no one has specified where they live, what they look like, where they come from....

The Girls

When I started my 'tour of duty' as a Caseworker in detention, I was assigned to a dormitory of twenty-four girls with whom to work. I had no experience working with girls, having always dealt with boys during my working years in other facilities prior to coming to detention. Since I was also a girl, I knew of my own concerns, worries, problems, questions and quandaries. This assignment was the beginning of on-the-job training, since at that time we were so busy and overcrowded that there was not too much time for measured, formal and observed guidance in working with the female population.

When I walked into the dormitory for the first time, I could read in the eyes of my charges, and in their expressions, that they had very little confidence in their new worker. In conversations with my co-workers about the residents, everyone always said that the girls have more needs, they are more emotional than the boys, they act out more, are more dramatic, they are more concerned about petty issues, etc., and are, in general, more difficult. Well, *we* are more emotional and seem to have a different set of feelings from the boys. Were these girls different from any other female because they were incarcerated? Not really. Many of the girls had children of their own and some were pregnant. Most decided to have their baby. Many of the girls had problems with their mothers, did not or could not relate to them, or their mothers could not or would not relate with their daughters, no less get ready for a baby on the way. In many cases, the mothers of the female residents knew that they would be raising their grands during the baby's beginning and neediest years, while their own daughters were completing time upstate and trying to get their own lives on track. Their own daughters needed a high school diploma, guidance, parenting classes and any other training and assistance that was offered.

In thinking back to my girls, I remember one fifteen-year old, pretty, petite girl, who was outgoing, talkative and very sensitive. This child almost had a child of her own, but had miscarried. I sensed that this was a very sad period in her young life. She wanted to have this child, loved the child's father and had suffered a loss. We spoke about loss, feelings, her future and her future children. I told her that although I had never lost someone so close as a child, I could identify with her feelings with the recent loss of my cat, who had died in my arms at the age of fourteen. I assured her that, of course, there was no comparison of loss, but I had an inkling of her feelings. She was ahead of me in many aspects of her life.

Several weeks later, she was placed in a group home, and with an onslaught of new admissions, she was pushed to the back of my consciousness. About a month later, she was back in detention, having been remanded to our facility by her judge, and I saw her on the stairs walking with her group. We recognized and greeted each other. She was again on my caseload, was doing well, and seemed a little more relaxed and happy than during our last contact. She was getting over her loss and in a sensitive moment on her part, she asked how I was feeling after my own loss, which was nice.

I interviewed another new girl who was thirteen-years old and had been arrested for prostitution. She was childlike, small and petite and easily led. She was crying during the interview, saying that she didn't do anything and didn't want to be locked up. She was sucking her thumb to pacify herself. She had been in placement in group homes and foster care, but wanted to go home, despite the fact that there were family problems at home. But there was nothing to be done until she went to court the following week for her hearing. She was beside herself with sorrow and tears and I referred her to our Mental Health Unit for supportive counseling. She completed the admission procedures, saw the Medical Unit for her admission physical and went to eat lunch after our interview.

I saw my girl later in the day walking with her staff, looking happy and content and with her hair fixed in a new style. She told me that she now felt comfortable in her dorm. She hopefully found some security and structure in detention.

It is not unusual for our residents to find positive experiences waiting for them in detention. No one invites them into our facility, but if they come to us, we try to offer them a new perception and perspective about their futures. They are like everyone else and feel things deeply, but are usually so caught up in their own concerns and difficulties of youth, they usually don't know how to verbalize feelings; but they do respond to kindness and empathy and will find ways to return the kindness.

I had a dormitory of twenty-four girls, a mixture of a variety of personalities, difficulties, of questions, problems and backgrounds, bubbling with feelings, fears and wonderings; but most important, while dealing with their court cases, families and other residents in their dorm, they were bubbling with their futures of possibilities and potential.

Belonging

There is an aspect of detention that seems to be known in the adult system as well as the juvenile detention system. Although they are two distinct and separate systems, with different rules, different incarceration times and a vast difference in age, one of the things that all detainees seem to share is the need to belong.

Children in juvenile detention are still children. They are exploring relationships, friendships, their own physical and emotional changes, changing hormones, missing family, peer pressure, the unknown, their hazy futures and any and every other puzzlements that children experience. They do have an added dimension in their lives that other teenagers in the community may not have experienced: the arena of alleged crimes, police, precincts, court, bookings, the bullpen and jail. What they are alleged to have done is not condoned, but they are still children who have the same needs, changing hormones, peer pressure…as others of their age group, of other children.

Many of the residents in detention have an inner need to belong to a group and they will associate with other members of a group, finding a kind of strength of family. Many go through an initiation of marking a part of their bodies as a manifestation of belonging. Some carry out a suggestion of assault, sustaining another charge on top of the charge for which they were originally detained.

One of my residents apparently felt a need for another family, although his mother was a lovely woman and loved her son. He had a little sister who was the pride of his heart. My boy had an inner strength noted by others not only in his dormitory, but in the entire facility. He was chosen to be a part of a group in detention and rose up through the ranks to be one of the group's leaders in the facility. He was very quiet and strong. He handled his long detention stay quietly, not asking for too much and taking what came to him. Things did come to him that might have been unfair, at which point he came to me for help and I did what I could for him. He was most relaxed when he had a special visit and bounced his little sister on his knee, or during our Family Days, when he could finally serve his mother and sister a barbecued meal in our large yard. He enjoyed giving back to them a little of the love and support that they had continued to offer him while he was in our facility.

I watched my boy during the year and a half that he was with us. I had watched him in the beginning when he was overwhelmed with pride at being chosen as the high leader in his group. I watched as he struggled to maintain a sense of order and control, how he interacted with the other residents in his dormitory, how quiet he always was, how he knew how to make things happen while continuing to be quiet and innocent. I watched as the responsibility began to overwhelm him. I watched him deal with many things, including missing his mother and sister, his court case, the possibility of doing time upstate, and his own maturing process.

If my boy pulled the strings of other residents and the others complied for their own reasons, if he did things that were not entirely positive or aboveboard, he received his returns in various ways. He took his comeuppance like a man. He only came to me for help if things got out of hand and his returns went too far.

My resident had many strengths, which may have detoured from the streets while he was in detention, meandering along the corridors, stairwells and offices, looking for security and belonging. He went through a year and a half of learning about himself and others, about his knack for leadership, and his ability to make things happen while others were often not even aware what was happening to them and around them. He was with us for an alleged charge and he went through his maturing process within the walls of confinement, within his own walls of the life that he had led and was now forced to look at. The pressures of detention were molding him and I knew he had the strength to endure. He was finally sentenced and was sent upstate to one of the secure facilities.

I kept track of my boy through the network that is woven by those who work with these residents. I learned that he was going to school upstate in the secure facility to which he had been transferred, that he had gotten his GED and was starting college courses. He had put aside the group he had been 'managing' in detention. New things were occupying his mind. Word was sent back to me from him to say hello and that he was fine. I know he will always be quiet and strong and will still be a leader because he has a quiet charisma.

I hope we were able to help him enough while he was in detention to allow him to continue to move ahead and be fine.

Escape

When my detention facility opened, it was a resource for the community; it was a place to house runaways and children in trouble for misdemeanors, mischievous acts and petty crimes. It was very rare that we received a youngster who was charged in Supreme Court with a very serious felony charge. Most of the residents were on remand from the Family Courts in all five boroughs. Even the structure of the detention building reflected the more relaxed attitude, accepting these residents as incorrigibles, who would eventually grow out of their mischievous ways.

As times and society changed, so did the nature and charges of our residents. We began to receive more hardened youths who were charged with different types of crimes, more serious and hurtful crimes. It is said that things often get worse before they get better, and we were on the slalom, going downhill fast, being inundated with Supreme Court remanded children who were being picked up for some of the more serious crimes in the City of New York.

The building had to change as well. Some years ago, the Juvenile Offender Law was passed, revealing that society was about to take steps to deal with this new wave of juveniles coming into the system. They would be charged more heavily and the young men who were over sixteen-years old could no longer place the blame for their illegal acts on a younger boy who would most certainly get a slap on the wrist and be released back to the community. It had been a pre-arranged plan and accepted by all parties who decided who would take the weight for the crime and how much it would cost the older boy.

The very next day after the Juvenile Offender Law was passed, trucks pulled into the sally port of the facility. Welders dragged out iron bars and welding torches, helmets and heavy gloves, and went to work putting bars up on every window in the facility. This facility was an eight-story building with an innumerable number of windows, and the workers worked and worked until they had barred up every one of them. Since the building did not have air conditioners, there was no space provided for them by the welders, and only years later, when the City brought in 'air' were the bars cut to accommodate the units.

The staff in detention made every attempt to keep the residents busy. The residents went to school from 9:00 A.M. until 3:00 P.M.; they had recreation which encompassed a large gym, swimming pool, a game room, weight room, radio, TV, movies and three yards. But…as busy and tired as the staff tried to keep the residents, the one thing that the staff could not do was to stop them from thinking.

I worked with the older male residents in detention, who ranged in age from fifteen to sixteen- years old. Some of them turned seventeen while waiting for the court cases to come to a disposition and resolution. They attended school, participated in all of the recreational activities that were offered, attended rap sessions, did crunches and lifted weights, played basketball, went swimming, played cards, checkers and chess and had their fights…but the staff did not know they were plotting and planning an escape.

The bars that had been welded to the window frame were on the inside of the window, accessible to the residents to lean on and peer through to the outside. During the summer months, the windows were opened behind heavy, thick screens that were behind the heavy, thick bars. Somehow, and I know it was not during their sessions in my office, although I would later be teased about it, they had arranged for a saw blade to be raised up on a lowered string, through a space in the heavy screen. Up, up it came, slowly on a moonless night, not to have a moonbeam shine on the metal and bounce off, alerting anyone to the scheme in progress.

Slowly, quietly, every night, they sawed the bars, just to the point of breaking, per so many of the movies they had watched that were supposed to keep them occupied and tired. One night, planned weeks ahead of time, three of my boys, in a dormitory of twenty-four residents, lowered the count to twenty-one. Sheets, tied together, were still swinging from the window in the slight summer breeze, the saw blade was found under a mattress and the separated bars were lying on the floor under the opened screen and cut bars.

This was a situation that could not be kept under wraps. It made the nightly news and the newspapers had a field day, with pictures and scathing articles about the inept system, the courts, the youths of today, the community, society, families and the Administration that had allowed these culprits to again infuse the community after they had been caught, charged, fingerprinted, handcuffed and led into detention. Investigations occupied the weeks following the escape and those staff on the front line in the dormitory, as well as the Administration, were held accountable.

How could my boys have left? We thought they were content, occupied, busy and tired. We forgot that there is nothing like home and that is the first place the police looked for them. Of course, in time, all were caught, one in Jamaica in the West Indies, one in his uncle's home and the third gave himself up. Each received a new escape charge and the time incurred on the new charge was added onto the time they faced on their original charges. They got what they had broken out for: they had their home-cooked meals, their mother's love, their family's warmth and any other warmth they managed to get while they were back in the community.

The staff had kept the residents busy and occupied, but did not know what they were thinking about in their rooms at night. We found out.

Celebrities In Our Midst

At times, I think back to the thousands of children who have passed my way during my years working in detention. Sometimes, images of the past start to reform and refocus in my mind and I remember the residents, their antics, their ways of being and if they were able to utilize the detention system as 'good time.'

One day, in the visiting area, where I was assigned to write passes for parents who were visiting their children, a gentleman approached the desk and said, 'I remember you. You were my Caseworker fifteen-years ago. I remember you looked out for me.' Of course, he had matured and had lines in his face that were not there when he was fifteen, but he and his story began to reform in my mind and I remembered him in my dorm. He added that I still looked the same, which was nice to hear.

Of the thousands, I sometimes think of the futures they will be creating for themselves; how much of an impact, hopefully a meaningful and important one, we have had in their lives; how their dreams are forming and materializing; if they have returned once again to the system; and how they see the world.

One of the questions I ask a new resident during his Intake Interview is, what his plans are for his future, or if he knows what he wants to be when he grows up. Many have not formed their dreams yet; most want to make money; some want to be entrepreneurs, not wanting to work for anyone else, not wanting to have rules or walls around them anymore; some say they want to be doctors (there have been a few future pediatricians) or lawyers (they do know the system from the inside out), and some want to be pro-ball players.

I worked with a few residents who were playing baseball on community league teams, where scouts meandered among the sandlots, searching for a potential big leaguers. One of my boys was a pitcher and another a shortstop. I spoke to the coach of my pitcher and it seems that this youth might be headed for a big league future. He must have had talent since the coach was going to sponsor my boy upon his being released back into the community. The shortstop had a determined quality about him, and he also played in a community league. He was a quiet youth, with a strong character, friendly disposition, and he liked people.

I told both of my niners that they would go on to bright futures, and they would forget all about me. They assured me that they would not, and would leave tickets for me at the Yankee Stadium box office.

I did not take any chances. I asked them both for their autographs, which tickled them, and I put them away with the notes I had taken on each. You never know.

Programs

A 'catch word' or an essential word associated with detention is the word 'programs.' The theory is to catch a youth in the net of prevention before he comes into the detention system. There has been a great deal of funding over the years to create and develop programs that deal with a youth and his family; programs that will deal with all of a child's free time, keeping him busy; programs that will involve and structure his family, molding a concern around him that will benefit all of his family members.

Some programs developed in the courts involve a child living at home, attending school every day, seeing his Aftercare Worker after school and having a curfew. The programs are very strict and very often a youth comes right back into detention having violated a term of his program, thus the term 'revolving door.' But they need to learn and a firm hand is very important.

Many programs are developed for prevention, to help a youth before he makes his way into the system; many are formed to help him after detention, to keep a very focused eye on a youth after he leaves a detention facility, and others have been created to work with residents who are in a facility. One detention program was comprised of actors who came onto the dormitories. They helped residents write scripts and directed them as they role-played their parts. Another program brought in more well-known film actors who worked on more scripts with the residents, but this time, they brought in a director who filmed the stories. The residents were able to see their efforts on an editing machine and they learned many skills involved in producing a movie. Another program involved a group who helped the residents role-play parts, again written by the residents themselves. The only problem was that the parts involved street activities…bum- rushing, simulating smoking, shooting, etc. I wonder if the residents learned something new that had not already gotten them into trouble. Many times, when I have escorted a resident along the corridors, he might see another resident down the hallway and pretend to aim and shoot. I quickly caution him that there is no shooting in the building, and that he is already in jail.

We had a program that dealt with Conflict and Anger Resolution. Many of our residents are in the habit of handling their frustrations and anger in a physical manner, acting first and then thinking about what they have done after they are counseled extensively. Along with this new program came a group of outgoing, assertive group leaders, who presented situations to our residents on the dormitories, asking for their input as to the best methods of dealing with situations, with the hope of reaching a positive outcome for the problems in non-physical ways. The group went to each dormitory, including the girl's dorm, presenting their scenarios, genuinely hoping to change behavior.

The tone in the dorms was generally quiet the day before this Conflict and Anger Resolution group came to help us. The residents went about their business, going to meals, relaxing in the recreation program, and attending whatever activity had been scheduled for them. There was no school since it was summer break. Time was spent in the yard, playing basketball, throwing a football around, playing handball or just enjoying some fresh air. It was a mellow time and staff and residents had time to relax, talk and counsel.

With the advent of this group, the air seemed to be infused with an unusual stress and anticipation. The tone in the entire facility was raised. It never ceases to amaze me how news spreads like a light beam in our facility as all of the residents were preparing to participate in the program. They were prepared alright! On every dormitory on which the Conflict Resolution group held its sessions, the atmosphere was altered and fights began to erupt. This occurred not only on one dormitory, but seemed to be like a domino effect, the dominoes toppling over behind these group members.

I attended one of the group meetings which was intended to reduce tension and teach better and more productive methods of dealing with frustration and anger, and I found myself more stressed than when I first came in.

Well, the Conflict and Anger Resolution group did its business on every dormitory, leaving a whirlpool in its wake. So much for some programs.

Culture Shock

Most of the residents in detention are a mixed lot in terms of culture. An intermingling of a variety of cultures, languages and customs is a great learning experience.

Detention is a small version of a melting pot and life on a dormitory is a small saucepan of a bubbling recipe…spicy, mellow, salty, hot, parboiled, quick to reach a boiling point…but always fresh to the palate, always interesting, arresting, different. It is a melt into which one can dip with interest, concern and empathy and come away with an expanded knowledge of a variety of cultures, customs, language and experiences. Once the residents are admitted into detention, their freedom is put aside for a while and they have no choice but to deal with others who may be different from their usual company.

Most of the residents I have gotten to know come to admit, although sometimes grudgingly, that coming into detention was the best thing that could have come across their paths. Their roads have already been trodden with all sorts of footprints of life experiences, many of which most adults never begin to experience. Some of the impressions in their paths are hardened to a stone-like consistency; the paths are often narrow, not letting any foreign undergrowth begin to get a foothold, or establish a new way of seeing things.

Being a captive audience, the residents in detention have no choice but to begin to get to know others in their dormitories. The barriers of newness and strangeness begin to break down since it is a natural human process to reach out for companionship from others. Nationalities, language and customs begin to fade as the inner human part of another is acknowledged. Alliances and allegiances begin to form and at times, the pendulum swings too far in the other direction, becoming residents against staff. The staff quickly straightens out that scenario.

Sometimes there is a staff member, generally a woman, who loves to cook and she shares her talent with the residents and staff in her unit. There is an 'elite lounge' which is akin to a small kitchen, complete with stove, oven, microwave, sink, refrigerator, etc. as well as tables and chairs. That staff may take some of the well-behaved residents to the 'elite lounge' and the feast begins to percolate. The smells begin to waft through the hallways, the air ducts, elevator shaft and stairways and everyone seems to manage to pass by the lounge to see 'what's cooking.' This is one area in which the various cultures come together in the anticipation and preparation of a delicious meal.

The kitchen training that the residents had at home begins to take form and they reveal themselves to be very creative cooks. They look professional, wearing rubber gloves and aprons. One of the Chinese boys I had in my dorm threw himself into one of the 'elite lounge' projects and created a special meal. Hot peppers, chili peppers and other hot, spicy items appeared as if from a gourmet magazine. The other residents joined in and the meal ranged from curried chicken to dumplings, sausages, three different kinds of rice and peas, brownies and corn muffins, to a punch that rivaled restaurant quality.

I was urged to try the delicious sausages cooked up by my boy, but was warned that it might be a bit spicy. I was fearless and did not want to appear scared or faint of heart. I should have heeded. I took a few bites of the sausage and the spicy sauce, which was really delicious, but more than I could handle. That is the time I had to run from the room to the nearest water fountain, and heard laughter drifting after my departure.

I am all for experiencing new things, different customs, languages and dress, but those hot sausages were too much culture shock for me.

The Swat Team

Because detention is a closed community, there are many things that go on that do not reach the outside world. Even the residents refer to their former lives prior to detention as…'when I was in the world.' Of course, there are occurrences that the Administration would rather keep in-house, as happens in any organization. These are 'family matters' that can be handled within the framework of 'family members' in the facility. There are plenty of incidents and situations in detention as there are in any large company, including births, passings of dear co-workers, retirements, get-togethers, hanging out, friendships, arguments, gossip and on and on. We all feel the same things.

And then there are the incidents which can only be described as awesome, funny, hysterical and any other adjective that can only begin to paint a picture of a completely different kind of experience.

One morning, as I reported to work, I walked through the scanner and through the two heavy doors that had to be 'popped' by Security in order to gain entry into the facility. In a second, and how this happens still remains a mystery to me, I could sense that the 'tone' in the facility was different. It was electric, excited, as if something were about to crackle in the air. Someone said something about people coming in to show us something different, some visitors who wanted to present new methods of structure and ways of handling and managing unruly 'inmates.'

I heard that something was going on in one of the yards. I looked out one of the windows that overlooked the yard. It was an invasion. There were police cars with their strobe lights rotating, throwing continuous, repetitive electric gleams along the facility walls.

Amassed in a row, along the fence, I counted at least seventy-five Correction Officers, all in an at-ease position, prepared to jump to attention at any second at the voice of their Commander. Many were wearing riot gear, replete with riot helmets, batons, bulletproof vests and boots, with their guns strapped down. It happened to be in the middle of summer and I know they must have been overheated in those outfits. From down the hall, I heard someone yell out something about dogs, and sure enough, two dogs jumped out of a car. This was just the beginning. We were in for something that was previously never done or experienced in juvenile detention. There was much more to follow.

After assembling for about a half-hour, the line of Officers began to file into the building. The tone of the building was still buzzing, especially in the dormitories where the residents were told that visitors were going to come into the dorms and show residents and staff 'how it should be done.' It should be mentioned that during this period of time, the residents were going through a phase of acting out. This is a phenomenon in detention that reflects a pattern based on the season of the year, holidays, weather and possibly a full moon. There are times that this kind of behavior can be predicted, but there are other times when the ebb and flow of emotions is just a 'human thing,' and not easily explained.

It was believed that the imposing presence of Correction Officers would present an impression of force, of strength, 'us against them,' to show our residents what they were in for if they did not stop their fighting and acting out on the dorms. It was a viable idea; after all, these are children in jail, not in summer camp or on an outing.

The line of Officers filed through the hallways, with the loud, echoing steps of their heavy boots, following their Commanding Officer, winding through the corridors, up and down the stairwells, in riot gear, heavy plastic shields down over their faces, helmets strapped under their chins, gloves, heavy bullet proof vests and canisters of something strapped to their legs. I was speechless and thoughtless. All of the Officers were big, strapping men, but the last Officer on the line was a woman, and she carried two tanks that I learned were filled with tear gas. There were armed to the teeth. This was a scene from a yet, unrated, unviewed B movie that left me breathless with laughter that was starting to bubble and gather in my deepest innards. The residents viewed this scene with a similar wide-eyed wonder, seemingly unaffected and unmoved by all of these tremendous efforts to impress with their serious attempts at intimidation.

Upon their entry into the dormitories, they showed the detention staff how a search 'should be done.' I think they went a little too far when they organized our detention staff into a single line, and Correction Officers and detention staff went marching through the corridors and up and down the stairwells. The only things our detention staff lacked was the riot gear, helmets, gloves, shields, vests, plus of course, the zealousness and seriousness of the Correction Officers. Our staff were also in wide-eyed wonder at the scene that was unfolding around them, a scene that had captured them within the walls of the directives of the Administration. Captured is the correct word, since staff was told that no one could leave the building during this exercise, even if their tour of duty was finished. We were virtually inmates as were the residents. There was much more to follow.

The lines of Correction Officers had broken off into sub-groups of camps, each with its own code name. The Command Center had been set up in the school library, which was on the fifth floor of the facility and each of the camps was in touch with one another by radio; and so I heard, 'This is 'C' Group...come in...come in...calling Delta Group... come in...come in...calling Blue Force...come in...come in.' The sub-groups had dispersed throughout the building, reporting to each other and to the Command Center.

Then I heard a bark from one of the corridors and I knew that the back-up team was on its way. After a few minutes, the Canine Unit came forth, sniffing its way along the corridors, into the dormitories, sniffing the chairs, rousting the residents out of the way, sniffing the rooms, in and out of the bathrooms, along the radiators, behind the TV and behind the staff desk.

The Canine Unit consisted of a German Shepherd and a black setter-type, a nondescript dog, but just as effectively trained as his brother. Suddenly, one of the dogs struck pay dirt in one of the radiators on the dormitory in which the oldest, largest boys resided, which happened to be my dorm. Since it was my dorm, I felt that I had license to go into the dorm to watch what was going on and I made my way through the dayroom, passed Correction Officers who were milling around, and into the residents' bathroom, where the action was. The focus of the Delta Dog was on the radiator, and sure enough, four force flashlights revealed a glint of metal buried in the deepest innards of the old radiator. A possible knife? A weapon stashed by one of the residents, to be used in a breakout? A weapon of protection? The Command Center was notified immediately of the find and the Captain found his way to my dorm to join the action, to join Delta Dog and Delta Force, and to give commands about releasing the gleaming, metal find from years of its imprisonment within the confines of the radiator.

Flashlights, levers and crowbars appeared from their stockpile of tools and one of the Officers began to dig and probe, reaching into and around the cast iron structure and pipes of the radiator. Happily, he shed his helmet, vest and other riot gear, only retaining his kneepads to save his knees from the hard bathroom floor. He probed and grunted, trying to free the metal object, but his flashlight only revealed that the find remained enmeshed and engulfed within the bowels of the ancient radiator. There was one bit of success. The heavy crowbar managed to dislodge the object about a half and inch, but there it stubbornly remained, refusing to be disturbed again. The Commander was observing the action and was reporting to the other camps scattered around the building of the progress, or lack thereof. I heard one of the Officers mention in frustration that maybe they should get their C-4 explosive, since their best efforts seemed to be in vain. I looked at him, trying to access the seriousness of his statement, hoping that he was joking. I continued to renew my license to remain on the scene and was right up in the face of the action in the bathroom.

Finally, after a frustrating non-successful effort at dislodging the object of the quest, the Commander made a decision and a call was put through to the Maintenance Department of the facility and the Director of Maintenance sent up his best man. Up came a quiet-spoken, very qualified member of the Maintenance team. He had experience in dealing with very difficult and challenging situations and he was known to remain calm in the face of adversity. He did not speak as he ambled along the main corridor. He did not need riot gear, vest, shield, helmet or even kneepads. The only tools he carried were his usual screwdriver and a pair of pliers that peeked from his back pocket. He face was a calm façade, knowing that all eyes were on him as he approached the combat area. He bent down over the culprit radiator, capturing the sight of the glint of the metal buried within, and took out his basic tools.

Within ten minutes, the object of everyone's concentration and frustration was liberated and an old, rusty, bent knife was held up for the Commander's view. The only damage that the rusty, old knife could have done was to create the need for someone to get a tetanus shot. Smiles broke out on sweaty faces, and the Commander radioed throughout the building to 'C,' 'Blue,' 'Green,' 'Silver,' and Delta Forces, that the mission was accomplished. The Correction Officers that had been observing the operation started giving each other high fives. The operation was over, the patient was almost blown up with C-4 and the rusty knife was finally liberated from its cast iron confines. I heard it was confiscated, bindled and tagged and placed in an evidence safe. The Commander, his combat forces, the Canine Unit, the tear gas canisters and the rest of the riot squad had completed its mission and marched in triumph along the main corridor, through the heavy doors and back into the yard, where they got into their vehicles, to return to their post, awaiting another call for their expert services.

The rusty culprit was not seen again. Apparently, it had been lying dormant in its radiator bed for the past fifteen years, waiting to be liberated. The facility used to provide metal silverware for the residents' meals, but that had changed to plastic-wear years before. A dinosaur from another age had been unearthed, not with crowbars, canisters, shields and masks, but with a screwdriver and a pair of pliers.

The staff was finally permitted to leave the facility after their tours had long ago expired. We had gotten a chance to see 'how it should be done' and we were glad the dogs had been properly trained so that no evidence of that day was left behind. It was one of those days and experiences that is etched in my mind and when I bring it back into focus and replay it, the happenings unfold as clearly as if it happened yesterday. I did appreciate the efforts the Administration took to try to teach our residents some realities they needed to learn, as well as the serious actions and tactics of the Commander and his Correction Officers; but the bubbling laughter and wide-eyed awe never fails me when I think of that day in detention. I hope others had as much fun that day as I did.

A Great Figure of Modern Times

Detention is a closed community where residents live, eat, sleep, do their chores, and more often than not, thrive. Aside from the detention staff who work with the residents on a daily basis, there are many caring people who come into detention from outside to work with the residents in the facility.

We have a chapel program, which serves every and any religion in the resident community. If the regular visiting church pastors do not meet the needs of the residents, other clergy and religious figures are invited in. We have hosted Muslim services conducted by an Imam, and I am proud to say that one of my former residents who was finally released home, was a member of that visiting Muslim group, and ministered to his former friends who were still in detention. I have also seen an Orthodox Rabbi, Baptist Ministers, Christian Ministers and Protestant groups, among others, who have ministered to our residents.

The Father who headed our chapel program was a man of letters as well as of religion. He was attending school to achieve his Master's Degree and intended to continue his education. I know because I typed a few of his term papers for him. I would not accept money for my efforts, but I hoped that he offered a few prayers for me instead.

Happily, he had a connection to one of the great figures of modern times and I was fortunate to be a part of this connection. He invited

Mother Teresa to come to our facility to meet with the residents in detention. I understand that she gladly accepted and my friend, the Father, told me about her visit. I made sure that my camera was in working order, after first making sure that taking pictures would be acceptable. I awaited the day of her arrival.

She came with two other sisters from her Order, the Sisters of Charity, as well as with a tall, pleasant gentleman, whom we assumed was her physician. We did not ask his position, but we knew that Mother was up in age and had suffered through a heart condition. She came in a car driven by her gentleman escort and a few of us met her at the heavy door in the lobby of the facility, which was quickly opened by our Security Officers. She was a tiny, tiny woman, her face full of smiles, very humble and grateful. She was dressed in the garb that we are accustomed to seeing her in, in pictures and TV, but in person, she brought a glow to her simple clothing. I took pictures and made sure that someone else took a picture of me with Mother.

I tried to take as many pictures as I could of Mother with other staff members, and would be giving each staff member a duplicate of the pictures. One of the Security Officers was so touched by her visit and by his picture with her, that he later asked me for an enlargement which he planned to send to his family in Peru.

I spoke with Mother Teresa and told her that I would like to send her copies of the pictures I was taking, and she seemed delighted with the idea. I also started to write to her after her visit and received letters back from her from India, which I keep in a special place.

We escorted her to the gymnasium, quite a large area, in which the viewing stands had been set up for the residents. Mother Teresa spoke to them. These boys and girls, who have experienced more in their few years than most adults, listened and watched her in awe. Although her message was special, it was not so much what she said, but there was something about her. She radiated an aura of warmth, understanding and love that filled the gym, and could have filled ten gyms with the same warmth and intensity. These street boys and girls were quiet and were at their most respectful behavior I have seen. Mother blessed us all with her presence. She and her sisters then handed out to each resident and staff member a medal that was blessed by her.

I cherish mine.

Heavyweights

The Recreation Department in detention has many contacts in the sports world, since many of our staff members who work in various titles in the facility, were themselves former sports stars.

I learned one day that Floyd Patterson would be coming to speak to the residents and I was prepared. I saw all of my residents, gave them their phone calls and helped them with any other concerns or needs they had (at that time, I was responsible for about twenty-five to thirty residents) in order to have all of my work done. I located my camera and got ready for his arrival.

Mr. Patterson is a very pleasant, quiet spoken gentleman who was gracious about wanting to speak to and help the residents. I was one of a few who was assigned to take him into the gym area where the podium and seats were set up, awaiting his arrival. As he came into the facility, and before he spoke to the residents, he turned around with a pained expression on his face and asked if anyone had any aspirin since he had a splitting headache. I said that I had some in my office and offered to provide him with the pain reliever. I escorted him through the corridors of the building and finally reached my office, surprising my supervisor who was in the area, and I introduced them to one another. I had my camera in tow and of course took pictures along the way.

After he took the aspirin, I escorted him back to the gym. He was a very down-to-earth person, without airs, and the staff and residents felt as if we had known him for a long time. He made all of us feel very comfortable. I took more pictures and made sure that someone took a picture of both of us and he went to greet and talk to the residents.

Sadly, we lost Mr. Patterson, a gentleman who wanted to reach out to others. A great loss to the sports world and to the rest of us as well.

The Greatest

Juvenile detention draws great visitors after arrangements are made, permission and authorization are attained, and phone calls, memos and a ton of other paperwork are completed and e-mails are sent. Administration recognizes the value and need for positive role models to come and meet with our residents and one of the staff members was given the assignment of making arrangements for important figures to come into detention to talk with us.

One day, as I was waiting for the elevator on the way to my office, the door to the interior of the building opened and a figure stood in the doorway. I had no prior knowledge of the arrival of this visitor and so the image and impression that remains in my mind as a stop-motion frame on a film strip, is of a huge figure looming in the doorway, taking up the entire frame of the door. (I realize that memory is often not exact and at times distorts reality).

The visitor was dressed in a suit and could not be missed. I recognized him immediately as Muhammad Ali and stood speechless from being in the presence of The Greatest, from not being prepared for his presence and from his heavyweight stature. I did not get a chance to hear him speak to the residents, but at the time of his visit, I was still new to the facility and did not have the know-how and a network of friends and co-workers that I developed as time went on.

After not being prepared or made aware of Muhammad Ali's visit, I made sure to keep my ear pressed to the floor, to the wall, to the grapevine or to any other fixture that would be a means of gaining information about the goings on in the facility.

I also started to have my camera on the ready, in order to put once-in-a-lifetime events into a form that could be touched, seen and remembered again and again.

More Heavyweights

One evening, I went to an agency function at which dinner was served. A fashion show was also in progress and awards were being presented. It was a long program, and I sat for a while in the lobby area, assisting the sponsors of the program by taking tickets and helping the guests check their coats. The line of visitors seemed to be endless, but they were gracious and smiling.

The gentleman checking the coats was well dressed, attentive to the guests and very polite and respectful, but appeared to be tired. A break in the visitor's line finally appeared, and I sat on one of the couches in the lobby area to take a brief rest. The cessation in the line resulted in the lack of activity in the coat checkroom and the gentleman came and sat down next to me. We started to talk and the conversation flowed as if we had known each other for a long time. I related my experiences in detention, working with the youths of New York City who had gotten into trouble. He was also involved with youths, but in the community. He lived about three hours away from the City and had driven in after work to volunteer his services to his friend who had organized the function. He said that he had to sit with his wife on a continuing basis to explain and fill in the gaps of his absences since he was always on the move with his community involvement, and he said that he especially missed his children. He took out his wallet and showed me pictures of his wife, a very attractive woman, and his beautiful little girls.

In addition to these commitments, I learned that he was a Reverend and he had a congregation to attend to. No wonder he was tired.

While he had his wallet out, he gave me his card, on which was printed The Fraziers, and at the bottom was a phone and fax number with the name Reverend Marvis Frazier.

We continued to talk about the function and about the youths of today, the reasons for their problems, the family's place in society, the breakdown of the family unit (into which he interjected his own guilt at being away from his family so often), and other social issues. He looked so tired and was not looking forward to the long drive back home that evening. He felt obligated to attend this awards dinner since he wanted to assist his friend in her first endeavor of a newly granted child care agency.

I was holding the card in my hand for about ten minutes, turned it over, saw a picture of two fighters in their fighters' stance, and then something clicked. I looked up and this gentleman suddenly looked familiar and then his name was familiar...Joe Frazier! I hadn't made the connection that this was the great fighter's son, who was also a fighter.

He did not seem to mind that I had not recognized his family name immediately; he was too down to earth for that. He did not seem to be impressed with titles, recognition or fame. He was more anxious to get his long drive home underway so that he could see his family.

The Tone

A very important word in detention that appears in much of the paperwork, incident reports and in the dorms' logbooks is the word 'tone.' It is difficult to describe this word in concrete terms, since it is not a word that creates a tactile experience. It is, rather, a vague kind of feeling word that gleans its meaning from the situation in which it finds itself.

This simple word can open caverns of unexplored sensations and tell one a great deal of what is going on or what is about to go on in an area or unit in detention. Ripples of airwaves, electrical charges, unseen by visual senses, can rip through a building in seconds.

I remember being on a subway once and the train was just leaving a station. All of the sudden, I heard, or rather sensed, an anguished cry that arose spontaneously from all of the people standing on the platform as well as those people around me. There was no conversation explaining what had happened. There was only a gut wrenching gasp that was an invisible story, telling that something awful had happened, an invisible tone in the station that communicated the fact that someone had fallen onto the tracks. Luckily, the train conductor perceived this unspoken message of distress and immediately applied the brakes.

Every dormitory has a logbook into which all communications, notations, incidents and log-ins are written by staff on the dorms. The Tour Commander, who makes rounds, traveling around the building to make sure all areas are functioning properly, makes a notation in the logbook indicating that the residents are involved in dorm activities, or are watching a movie, or playing board games or cards, and that the 'tone is good.' This, in fact, means that there were no physical altercations, arguments, or other dissentions in the group, that the residents were relating well to one another at that point in time. That point can change in seconds.

A 'high tone in the house' indicates that staff on all dorms must be on their toes since dissention in one area can spread like wildfire in seconds. How does one side of a large, meandering building 'know' what the other side is doing? Perhaps by osmosis? It is difficult to figure out the means of communication since it cannot be seen; it occurs faster than one can share information by phone and it falls within the arena of spontaneous combustion, an explosion of sorts with invisible grapevines of ripples and currents.

There is nothing better than the way invisible intertwinings, meandering grapevines along which the impulses of gossip, information, news, the impending arrival of important visitors, new rules and regulations, and of course, 'the tone' are transmitted throughout the building.

It is better than e-mail. Not everyone has access to a computer and the only receptors needed to access the impulses are one's senses.

The Rap Session

Most of those who work in the field of juvenile detention care for the children in our confines. We know that they are mere children, and we realize that their psyche is still childish because they have not yet had the years of experience to teach them otherwise. We also know that they have been out 'in the world,' a world that most people have not experienced and most likely will not experience in their lifetimes.

Although they can be as natural and in some ways as innocent as a kitten, they can also be mischievous, negative, demanding, intimidating, aggressive and argumentative. The hardened layers of the streets have not yet been peeled back by our staff. The staff working in a detention facility is, for me, one of the highlights of a resident's stay. The resident has access to the recreation areas, the yards, the gym, chess, cards, board games, quiet time and school... but these activities do not compare in my mind, to the caring qualities of the staff who work directly with the residents, who work 'on the line' every day.

The staff can be rough with the children, as rough as the streets have been rough. The staff has to deal with a large number of residents in a dormitory. Many staff have been in the military and are accustomed to a structured environment and believe that a strict, firm tone lends itself to an appropriate counseling situation for these youths. Many staff have worked in similar settings, such as the Corrections system, and they bring their own variety of structure to detention.

Since the ratio in detention is a high eight residents to one staff member, the staff use a variety of methods for the purpose of handling the group in the most positive manner possible.

One of the means of change and counseling in the dormitory is the rap session. The talent and caring of the staff can be manifested in this arena. Many are articulate, confident and have a sense of humor and it is almost like attending a special show to hear some of the staff counseling during the rap sessions. They can be tough and rough and hard as concrete, but they are just acting in their roles of surrogate parents to our residents: 'You want to be a man, be a man, take care of your own. In case you don't know it, you're in jail. You're used to having your mother pick up after you? Pick up after yourselves. I know your houses aren't a pig sty, so why do you treat your dorm, your living space, like a pig sty? Why should I have to thank a resident for picking up someone else's snotty tissue? Pick up your own snotty tissue! You use a game? Put it away. You move the chairs all around? Put them back! Guess what. You can complain all you want to about the rules, but remember, if you're hear for six months, for a year, I'm going to keep on saying the same things until you get it. You're supposed to go out there to show the world something. Like it or not, this is the way we're going to hold this house down, and you new jacks are messing up our house. When you all start getting rowdy out there in front of the TC's and the Supervisors, I'm going to straighten you out. Everyone's not going to deal with your nonsense, and you reflect this dorm. You got a beef with someone, you come to the staff! You don't handle it yourself! Anybody got anything you want to say? And last, but not least, I've got some music videos, then we have the yard and after showers, we have a movie.'

There is a variety of rap session methods and the above example may reflect the need of staff to deal with an immediate problem in an immediate way, such as a rising tone, the residents talking out of turn, raising their voices or too many getting up out of their seats without permission. These types of potentially negative behaviors have to be nipped in the bud before they blossom into a bouquet of fragrant, pungent, earthy fights.

I have also experienced a different type of rap session in which all of the residents and staff sit in a circle and all those participating have to look at each other. I remember one in which everyone had to say what was the most anxiety-provoking situation that had occurred that week. Since I was a part of the circle, I had to participate as well. This was a helpful method and brought all of us together, feeling a common 'feeling bond,' although most of us in the circle were not used to sharing feelings in front of a group.

The Rap Session is a viable counseling tool that can address group concerns. Residents can hear questions and anxieties of others and may not feel so alone in their quandaries. They can sit and watch skilled speakers who try to impart their experiences to those who are in many ways still innocent.

The common vein that runs through all sessions, talks, counseling and tough love, is the desire to peel back another tough layer already set by the cement of the streets.

The Squeeze

It is inevitable that residents get into trouble in detention. After all, they are accustomed to the rough streets that scrape at them, that throw them up against the hard walls, scratching at them so that they are scarred, sometimes for life.

As much as the staff is with the residents twenty-four hours a day, working in three shifts, and as much as the residents are under observation at all times, these are residents who have learned to slip and slide under a watchful eye, and they are as quick as they can be at doing what they want to do.

The residents are involved in many activities in all parts of the building and enjoy a full recreation program. In addition to basketball, cards, chess, board games, play stations, TV, tapes, radio, movies and other activities, they also have access to ping-pong and other table games. The staff has to be extra diligent in monitoring some of the games, which used to include pool. However, since the pool sticks were, on occasion, swung like a bat and a pool ball, on occasion, was secretly packed into a sock to become a dangerous weapon, the game of pool was removed from detention. Before pool became a thing of the past, staff had to be aware of how many pairs of socks a resident was wearing, especially if the group was scheduled to play pool. Staff is wise and alert; a chain of deduction involving socks occurred, and the culprit would be stopped in his tracks before an incident occurred.

There was an instance when a pool ball was missing. This may sound trivial, but in detention, this is a major situation, and all activity in the building was interrupted and came to a stop. A major search was launched by Security, which sifted through all residents' personal belongings as well as all areas of the facility itself, until the ball was located in the gym area, in the toilet paper dispenser.

Sherlock Holmes could not have done a better job in tracing the ball, mapping out a trail of its travels, short of taking fingerprints, and the blazing trail ended at the doorstep of my dormitory. It seems that my boys were the only ones to be scheduled for gym that afternoon and they were the only ones who had been in the vicinity of the pool tables. How someone slipped the ball off the table, leaving an obvious space in the rack of balls; where it was stashed; who would have been the intended one to end up with a lump on his head or worse...were questions that remained a mystery.

There were more subtle questions that were raised: others may have seen the ball being taken, but depending on the pecking order, aggressiveness or stature of the culprit, the others may not have dared to say anything. Detention is a small, closed society, and as in outside society, there are many levels of life, survival and behavior that are operating simultaneously.

The staff was obligated and determined to find out who took the ball. They knew that it did not develop legs and open the heavy metal doors that are opened only with a big key. One of the methods that is commonly used as a tool in detention is peer pressure, which is a viable method given the number of residents in a dormitory. All of the residents were held accountable and responsible for the incident and although most may have been innocent, all were read the riot act.

'I'm going to find out who did it,' said a Supervisor, matter-of-factly, as if it were already a done deal.

After the group of residents was counseled by staff, the residents were left to ponder and wonder, and the pressure started to build. They became angry at being punished for something someone else had done, and started looking around with accusing glances at the others in the dorm. There was an uneasy and suspicious tone in the dorm. The Supervisor knew that someone would crack and spill the beans. The Squeeze was on!

This is a method that is usually foolproof; it always works; the culprit cracks and the punishment, which would certainly be a behavioral level drop, would be easier to swallow than dealing with the pressure being applied by the forces that were surrounding him in the faces of the other residents.

However, there is always an exception to a foolproof rule.

For some reason that cannot be explained, this mystery was never solved; the perpetrator got away with his deed and was a silent martyr to the cause of not cracking under pressure....silent because his identity was never discovered.

As a result, the pool tables were removed from the facility, the pool balls and sticks were packed away and the routine of counting of socks was put on hold.

Nicknames

Many of our residents are known by names other than those names that were pinned onto them when they were born, that is to say other than their 'government names.' Some of the names describe physical characteristics, others describe an essence of a person, but most of the names that follow someone seem to be appropriate and many remain with him all of his life.

I looked up the word 'nickname' in the dictionary and read: a descriptive appellation added to or replacing one's actual name, and then looked up 'appellation' and read that it is a name or title. But the word that I like best is the simple 'nick,' a shallow notch or indentation on a surface. This is just what a nickname is: a surface, glancing blow, missing the larger physical target of a person, but grabbing the essence of him in one or two words.

I have heard a large variety of nicknames that the residents call each other or call themselves. They don't generally tell in an interview what their nicknames are, but during phone calls, they may drop the hint when they identify themselves to the party on the other end of the phone. I have heard, 'This is...Slim, Tubs, Pin (for a boy who had a pin in his leg from a car accident), Fish, LaLa, Poopie, Poppi, Dynamite, Dice, Limpy, Muchie, Scarface (for a resident who had an unfortunate razor scar on his face from a fight), Mini-me, Monster, and others. There are times I hear a resident called a nickname and I wonder what I have missed in him or I wonder what he had been doing 'out in the world' to garnish such a special name, which captured such an intrinsic part of him.

There are times one goes on for years and does not know a person's real name, but knows him only by his essence, his nickname. Very often, the detention staff is also known by nicknames, or more often, by first letters of his or her last name, such as Ms. B, Ms. G, or Mr. O, and one does not bother to learn or pronounce the rest of the name.

After years of being called by my proper, given name, I finally got a nickname. I don't know why it took me so long to get mine. I only know that it makes me feel special. No one has a name like it. I didn't know what I had been missing until finally, someone caught my essence.

Revenge

From the way many of the residents in detention talk, they know almost everyone in Brooklyn, or in the Bronx, or whatever borough they may call home. Everyone is 'watching my back,' or is 'my man' or 'my homey' or 'my son' or 'is under the wing,'or has his own 'crib' and is 'living large' or is 'good money.' They have it all covered, with a network that reaches in and out of every street, up and down every stairway and up and around every corner and park of the City.

This is not necessarily so. The residents are children, and still have a child's way of seeing life. They like to see themselves as the center of their world, as the focal point of their friends, as the most vital and important contact person in their hood, the one others must seek out. They have many acquaintances, but few genuine friends, and we tell them that if their friends were really friends, they would not have led them into an arrest and detention situation. Children this age have such a need to belong to others that their view of their already fragile world becomes even more distorted.

The reality of their world, their running and dodging, their perception that the streets are more important than school, their belief that their friends are more important than their families, their belief that they run a network of contacts through which they believe they run their neighborhoods is actually a fine spider web of mistrust, anxiety and confusion. They may think that their web can catch any rumor that may be floating, advising them to watch their backs; they may believe that a potential recruit may be paralyzed for the moment, caught in their web of their control, but they are actually caught in the web of their own confusion.

Very often, 'friends' or co-defendants become frightened when they are caught, and with the influence and persuasion of the authority figures and with the immensity of the Court system looming over them, they quickly and willingly 'give up' or snitch on their 'friends.' This may lead to complicated ramifications. The one who snitched is outside 'in the world,' while the one who was snitched on, left to hold the bag, is in detention.

Along with the busy activities that keep him occupied all day: school, recreation, programs, rap sessions…he also has time to think of his predicament and the events that led him to become involved in the detention system and about the one who snitched on him.

What a resident thinks about while he is in our facility is of the utmost importance. He has choices: he can go on as he was prior to his admission, he can begin to listen to the seemingly endless counseling, or he can become embittered and angry, and all of the frustrations he felt from his former, frayed life can become embroiled within him. He may vow revenge on those whom he feels betrayed him and gave him up.

I was working with a youth who was in detention for about eight months and who was on continued remands from the court, which was trying to determine the best plan for this resident. He had been in foster care since he was a small boy because his mother was unable to care for him. She had remained in the picture, however, and she was beginning to re-enter his life with positive plans for herself and for her children. She was getting herself together.

My resident began to respond to a new nurturance form his mother that he had missed for many years. In addition, he began to respond to the consistent, constant, structured atmosphere of detention. He stopped fighting, stopped reacting in an overly sensitive way to everything that was said to him, and he began to write poetry. He revealed a talent which even he was unaware he possessed. He continued to call his family and was happy to reach his mother by phone, and she began to visit him. She was trying her best to make a change in her life.

When a resident is making a phone call, he and his conversation are monitored by the Case Manager. Most of the time, we go on about our paperwork while he is on the phone, paying attention, but not really paying attention, to his conversation. When he begins to talk in a softer voice is when we become more attentive, but continue to go about our paper and computer tasks. If he becomes inappropriate, if he is planning revenge, or becomes negative, he receives our full attention and his conversation is interrupted. Politeness is forgotten. He is in detention to learn, to be counseled, to change, to begin to peel off those layers of street, toughness and not caring. I have had to stop many conversations.

My eight-month resident had received his court papers from his attorney. Within the court papers were all of his charges along with the statements of his witnesses and co-defendants. This receipt of papers from an attorney begins a chain reaction and a re-emergence of old, negative and angry habits, which had been pushed to the back of this youth's mind. In detention, he had begun to participate in positive activities; he was becoming more open and sharing of his concerns, and many of his former negative impulses were being replaced by more productive thoughts.

He learned from the court papers that his co-defendant had snitched on him and he began to plot and plan revenge. During a phone call, he began to recapture his former negative thinking and a domino thought process was quickly leading him backwards to his old ways. His phone call was interrupted. Counseling began immediately, to strike while the iron was hot, while he was in his regressive mode. Counseling involved talking about letting go of negative, vengeful thoughts… thinking more positively…thinking about a positive future…letting the past go…'you were a boy then, you're a man now, almost 17… you're too mature for that old way of thinking;' basic, down to earth ideas aimed at his mind; an arrow aimed at the target of his thoughts.

The next day, he said that he had been thinking about what I had said to him, of the possible consequences of his potential negative, vengeful actions. He visualized the consequences of those thoughts and took them through a myriad of situations that could result from such actions. He decided to put aside those negative thoughts and actions and gave me the reasons why.

I could feel his struggle not to let his former, negative and unproductive thought patterns and habits take hold again and overrun him, and he had to push them back down to a holding cell in his mind. 'It will be easier the next time,' I told him.

He grew up before my eyes. I'm glad he was able to listen.

Bi-Products

Working in detention is a challenging job. There are many rules and procedures to follow, as there is in any large organization. There are many different personalities in a facility, and we are all mandated to focus on our main responsibility of caring for children. There is a great deal of paperwork, e-mails and reports that must be produced for the courts, records that must be maintained and kept up-to-date, and each worker must answer to a supervisor, as exists in every organization.

Working with the children is the easy part.

The staff is always trying to take any situation and make it a learning experience for a resident. I was eating in the dining room one day at dinnertime and the residents were also eating their evening meal. The staff does not always eat, since they must be alert at all times, or they choose not to eat if what is being served is not to their liking. They often order out or eat out on a rare break. One of the residents had eaten quickly and wanted to get up to empty his tray, asking permission from a staff member first. An opportunity for counseling! Counseling in this situation involved showing respect for others and not hurrying others who were still eating. These were patterns of behavior for him to remember and to apply to his family when he eventually went home. That resident liked being mentally and psychologically 'restrained' in that moment. He had a concerned, strong adult to give him attention and teach him something, and he appreciated it, which could be seen in his facial expression.

Another of my residents was in a sad state of affairs, not of his own choosing, but his life was the result of things not falling into place for him. His mother loved him dearly, but she had her own issues, and landed up in a shelter. He had not heard from her for months and was feeling anxious, desperate and lonely. He did not know who his father was and his brothers and sisters were scattered among a variety of foster home agencies. He felt abandoned and neglected.

I started to make contacts and fortunately ran into a few caring and helpful people in other agencies. I gathered phone numbers and contacts, all for the purpose of finding my boy's mother. It paid off and after leaving a message for her at what I hoped was my final call, I got a call from the mom. I put her on hold while I went to get her son. I did not tell him who was on the phone, but got a kick out of watching his face light up when he heard his mother's voice. That led to his mother going to court for him, visiting him, and within two weeks, he had been accepted into a program, with his mother involved, and once again vital in her son's life.

A couple of days before my boy was to leave, he asked to speak to me and came into my office. 'I want to thank you,' he said, 'I wouldn't have been able to find my mom without your help. When I make my future, I won't forget you. Thank you.' He held out his hand to shake mine. It couldn't have gotten better than that!

Another of my boys had already contacted his family during his weekly phone call, but asked to speak to me. I know that when a resident asks 'to speak to me,' he doesn't want to 'speak to me,' he wants a phone call. This resident felt a need to call his family to ask them something pertaining to court or clothing for his court appearance, or any other reason he could think of to speak to his people.

'No problem,' I said, and he came into my office and made his two or three minute call. He appreciated it, raised himself up to his full height of six feet, put on his best manner and said, ' 'Thank you <u>ever</u> so much.' I smiled and said, 'You're <u>ever</u> so welcome,' and he smiled back. A new connection of respect was forged in that moment.

What terrific feelings! These are bi-products of a process, the excess of daily tasks that is caught in the run-off. These vignettes are not the main purpose of my job, which is to do the best of my ability to help these residents adjust while they are in detention, to help them try to change their lives, contact their families and lawyers and to help them grow up emotionally.

Helping the residents and working with them in detention is easy. The bi-products of appreciation, respect and caring is an unexpected bounty that enriches an already fulfilling job.

Prom Night

Have you ever seen a transformation, a metamorphosis before your very eyes?

A new program, called the Leadership Program, was started by one of our innovative directors, which took place during the summer months. This program filled in the school-less days for the residents so that they would stay involved and not left to their own devices and thoughts. Involved staff offered classes in Art, Music, Social Skills, Interview Skills, Health, Sports, and any other interest or skill that a staff member had to offer in an area where a resident was able to benefit. I worked with a few girls teaching them to crochet.

The finale of the summer was a presentation of all those skills that had been developed during the summer months. Displays of artwork and skits were presented in the gym, poetry was read, dancing and singing were recorded and everyone was cheered and applauded for their efforts and courage to get up in front of the whole 'house.'

At the start of the summer program, one of the staff members had organized a group of residents, including both boys and girls, and worked with them on a daily basis in the cafeteria during off hours when meals were not being served. She and her team began to teach the group of residents about manners, etiquette, social skills and respect. Many of the residents who were recruited had been presenting their usual behavioral problems on their dorms. They were selfish, acted out, started fights and were disrespectful to staff, using profanity freely. Counseling on the dorms was on-going to try to correct and improve this behavior, but changes often take a long time. We wondered how the staff of this special program was going to polish these particular residents in a short period of time before the final day. As we walked by the cafeteria during our daytime tasks, we noticed that the residents involved in this project were not acting out, were attentive and seemed to be involved in the program.

The finale of the summer program arrived. We enjoyed the skits, dances, poetry and songs in the gym where bleachers had been set up, and waited for the last part of the program with bated breath.

Chairs and tables with white tablecloths, cutlery and plates were moved into place on the gym floor. A single flower stood in a vase on each table. The lights were lowered, and suddenly melodious, sophisticated, soft club music began to stream over the speakers. From the back door of the gym, a procession of transformed residents began to walk slowly to their tables. The loud, boisterous boys were now wearing suits, ties, some wore vests, and all had polished shoes. The difficult, seemingly non-caring girls were now resplendent in floor length gowns, walking on the arms of the boys who were escorting them to their chairs. Their beauty and self-esteem in those moments were reflected on their faces.

They walked slowly; the boys guiding their ladies to their seats, holding out their chairs and helping them into the chairs; calm, well-mannered, sophisticated. We couldn't believe our eyes. At a soft music cue, the couples got up to dance a slow fox trot; the scene was reminiscent of the days of grand ball rooms, etiquette and manners.

The transformation was astonishing. The metamorphosis was total. The residents themselves got a chance to see themselves in a new light, a new setting, with respect and a new outlook. With hope, some of the transformation was imprinted in their on-going need and search for stronger self-esteem, self-value and potential.

Family Day

Juvenile detention is a completely different world and concept from Adult Corrections. The theory and practice for juveniles in jail is based on the fact that residents in detention are still children, with a child's outlook, fantasies and misperceptions. The reasons for their being detained, their alleged accusations, are far from being condoned; but what else is there to do but try to help them change their lives so that they can have a choice of a better life style in the future. We really have no choice but to give them a choice and a chance. The alternative is to punish without rehabilitation, to censure without teaching, to accept them without trying to help them change their lives.

When those 'in the world' hear about all of the 'advantages' of being in detention, I have heard that some get arrested just to be in our facility. In reality, they crave structure rather than running rampant, emotionally and physically, in the streets. We have a full program of recreational activities, school and family contacts and visits. What kid wouldn't like all that?

One of the activities that is scheduled on a regular basis is Family Day. This project is a big one in terms of organizations, e-mails, food, charcoal, grills, tablecloths, decorations, large trash bags, basketballs, volleyballs, balloons, music, raffles, snow cones, cotton candy...and last not but not least, a request for a beautiful, sunny, day, with very little wind so the paper plates, cups and napkins will remain in place.

For some reason, the organization for the first Family Day in juvenile detention history was placed right in my lap. We utilized the large yard and each dormitory made a large banner welcoming the guests. I still have pictures of the colorful tables, barbecue grills, balloons, children playing and residents having a ball with their families. The residents felt an urge to serve their families, balancing plates of food and cups of juice, napkins and plastic ware for their family members. They stood on the barbecue line with their little brothers and sisters, filling their plates with ribs, franks, beans, chicken, hamburgers, salad, pickles and chips. A few of the food service staff manned the grill, some of the staff served the buffet lunch, the weather was perfect and all was well in detention that day.

Our residents rose to the occasion of playing perfect hosts. There were no incidents and there was no acting out behavior. There were a few youths whose families could not make it to the occasion, and the staff tried to help them put aside their forlorn looks, frowns and feelings of being neglected on this special day.

Some would question the purpose and validity of having such activities and programs for those in juvenile detention, for those who have allegedly committed crimes against families and communities. If a positive program is offered which presents a different vision and perspective to a youth, an activity during which a resident can learn a new way of handling himself positively in a social situation, it can only have positive results.

It is worth spending the extra money on balloons, tablecloths, franks, chicken, beans, charcoal, pickles and chips. Many times, the staff chips in, buys the goods and materials and does not put in a personal expense for reimbursement of the funds. The tasks are done with caring for the residents, in an attempt to show them new choices, a new way of life, and connections and re-connections to their families.

Juvenile detention is, for the most part, for most of the residents, a last chance, a last stop; applying brakes in a downhill spin that has gotten out of control. At this point, when their lives have reached the seriousness of a detention situation, we really have no choice but to try to help them build a more solid and positive structure for their lives.

It's All About Respect

Many of our residents come into detention fresh from the street. Although most come from homes with very caring parents, it's the street persona that first strikes our staff when residents are admitted to our facility. Aside from being accustomed to doing what they want as they are running the streets without guidance, and aside from not caring at the moment what they get themselves into, they are scared, they can be aggressive, argumentative and intimidating.

One of my residents was only fifteen, but he stood six feet two inches, had a full beard and had a very assertive and argumentative demeanor. His MO was to bully to get what he wanted. He was a dorm leader, but often misused his leadership skills negatively, either to stir up other residents or to intimidate and bully them to get his way.

He tried to use his methods on me. He went about it in a round-about way, by telling other residents to get off the phone or not make their phone calls so he could make his. He tried to intimidate them and his subversive threats often worked...for a little while.

One day I went to the dayroom of the dorm, went to my boy and crooking my finger, said, 'Come'ere, I want to talk to you. He came to my office and I told him, 'Sit down,' and I gave him 'the talk.'

'Who do you think you're dealing with?' I asked him. 'Who do you think you're talking to? You don't tell anyone anything and you don't tell me anything! I tell you!!' A minute or two was enough and at the end he said meekly, 'OK,' and left the office.

The next day, he greeted me and said, 'You're the best Caseworker! You're my best friend!'

But he wasn't through. He liked attention, and when I asked another resident if he wanted to make his call, my boy acted offended. After all, he was a dorm leader and he was being by-passed. So, when the other resident completed his phone call, I went up to my boy, looked up at him and asked him, 'I would like to extend a personal invitation to you to see if you would like to make your call now.' He smiled at the game and came to the office.

A week later, he came to make his call and had a pen. He started to write on the desk and I cautioned him about what he was doing and he stopped. Then, while he was on the phone, his pen in hand headed towards the wall and I again cautioned him not to write on the wall. He stopped, but started to aim again at the desk.

I said, 'I'm going to take the pen away from you,' and I would have.

And he would have let me.

Now, that's respect. It's all about respect in detention.

Hair and Sneakers

Teenagers pass through a myriad of phases, and just because they are in a detention situation, does not mean that they don't pass through these stages as well as those who are 'out in the world.' Of the many manifestations of those teenage years, two of the more obvious and telling are hair and sneakers.

Through the network and grapevine that sends its tendrils from detention into 'the world' and back, the hair and sneaker styles change inside as they do outside. Through viewing TV and from phone calls and visitor contacts, the residents are kept up-to-date about everything from preferred underwear, hats, jackets, pants, sneakers and shirts; and they want their mothers to buy the latest styles for their court appearances. Even though they are in detention, they are still children in need.

I have had some residents order clothing from the attached order forms that often fall out of magazines. When their mothers were charged, there was an uproar and of course, a new procedure was born. If a resident received a magazine through the mail, we were to tear out all of the order forms and have the magazine signed by the supervisor before it was put into the residents' hands.

I have seen hairstyles pass through so many style changes that I have lost count. From 'fades' to 'caesars' to 'baldies' to 'bowl' cuts to 'military cuts,' 'braids,' 'box braids' to 'puffs' and on and on. Desired sneaker styles change as well, and at times, there is pressure put on mothers to get new styles and colors as soon as they hit the stores.

One of my boys who had been in detention for over a year and a half was growing up with us, and as expected, he was going through his teenage stages of rebellion as he would have done if he had been living at home during this period of his life. The focus and manifestation of this particular youth's rebellion, growth and development was his hair. His hair was undulatingly wavy and long. As his stay with us progressed, he had his hair cut by the barber and then he began trying different styles: a caesar, a 'mohawk,' a spiky style, a bowl style that we see in old Western movies, and finally a fade, in which a three inch area along the sides and around the back were almost shaved off, leaving the top, which he had parted in the middle, overflowing over the empty areas.

His first brush with the stir that his haircut caused was when his mother came to visit him. 'Oh, no!' she said. 'You can't go to court like that and I don't like it!' The haircut inspired the same reaction in his father, grandmother, grandfather and last but not least, his attorney. His attorney, who was already overworked and under stress, said that his blood pressure shot up when he saw his client. 'What the heck is that!' he exclaimed. Needless to say, the do would not do.

I had to tell my boy my honest opinion as well, which was that I did not like it either. We discussed different hairstyles that would be preferred for a neat, clean-cut court appearance, and he settled on waiting for the 'fade' to grow in, at which time, he would go for a natural, more acceptable cut. He did not want to give up his striking out at independence and rebellion, but on the other hand, he knew the reality of his situation. He also did not want to alienate his lawyer, mother, father, grandmother, grandfather and social worker.

One day, his group went to the barbershop and I almost panicked, but thought, 'No, he wouldn't get a new extreme cut.' When he returned to the dorm, I was relieved to see that his haircut had not changed.

'So,' I said, 'You didn't get a haircut, right?'

He smiled and assured me, 'No, I just got a shave.'

The Cache

All aspects of humanity are reflected in detention. It is a cache of humor, feelings, emotions, caring....a vein of untapped, rough gemstones winding their way through a mountain of order, rules and structure.

The humanity reflected in detention is evident in all those who are confined within the walls of the facility, for we are all really locked in. The staff has keys to move within the building, but the doors leading to the outside are fitted with a different key, which is in the sole possession of Security. It takes time for some of the staff to become accustomed to being in detention, and many feel that closed-in feeling for some time.

One of the veins of this society is the facility school. The residents are required to attend school on a daily basis and if they refuse, they are counseled and may lose a level on the behavior management program. A higher level means more privileges, more phone time, a later bedtime and more commissary. The teachers reach out to the residents at their level, not the level of being skipped for social reasons, but at their actual reading and math grade levels. The residents are tutored and receive individualized attention, and many seem to catch up quickly. At the end of the year ceremony, which is the school graduation, the parents are invited to attend to see their children receive certificates of merit and hear their speeches. These are honors that many never achieved before in the community. Photos later reveal the glistening tears of pride in the eyes of the parents who almost gave up hope for their lost children.

All those who counsel the residents are sure to emphasize school as a priority within and without the detention walls. The minds and desires of teenagers meander to all topics, quests, wonderings, wanderings, daydreams, plans and questions. They often become lost in their dreams and put aside reality for a while. All those who counsel the residents recognize this tendency, often from our teenage years, but we bring them back to reality. The reality and importance of school and education is constantly stressed. The outer society and the smaller society within the walls of detention require that school be an important topic of conversation to be discussed at every and any opportunity, until it vibrates in a resident's thoughts and being.

We have keys to move around the facility, to escort the residents to their respective planned activities and programs. We also have keys to open a resident's mind, to reach in and nourish this untapped vein of humanity.

Scars, Tattoos and Other Markings

One of the things that cannot be taken away from a resident is his ability to think, ponder and be creative during his free time. The residents are generally kept busy during the day with school, which they attend from 9:00 A.M. until 3:00 P.M., recreational activities, which includes utilizing the gym, the yards, or hall time when they play cards, chess, board games, read, talk, watch videos or play games on the play station.

A detention day is filled with the usual activities of a teenager, including school and recreational activities. In addition, the resident is making alliances with other residents in his group; they talk about what will happen in court, they compare cases while trying to crawl in to the mind of the judge to see what may happen on the next hearing date, they compare 'war stories' of the streets; they are 'watching their backs' and gathering forces among the other residents who will watch their backs for them when they are not watching their own backs. The need to belong is very compelling for all of us.

Some residents feel an urge to affiliate themselves with a group… believing in power in numbers. Some want to announce their affiliation by marking themselves with the patterns or special codes of their group, perhaps with the hope that a mere look at a marking will make an aggressive resident with unsavory intentions think twice about making a move against him. To a resident, this might not sound like such a bad idea. However, this type of activity is taken seriously in detention, resulting in further counseling about anger management, future goals, maturity, etc.

I don't think our residents deserve to have to prove their worth through aggression, unsavory intentions, markings or mere looks. They are and can be so much more.

Security

In detention, Security plays a large part of the make-up of a secure detention facility. We have a group of Security Officers who are overworked, understaffed and multi-taskers, who have done many doubles over the years. They respond to distress calls within minutes by running through the hallways, up and down the corridors and stairwells, and they have sometimes commandeered the elevator in an emergency.

They search the residents after visits, since at times, things get passed from visitor to resident, in which case, the visitor is restricted from further visits for a period of time. They monitor the visiting area and their presence is a reminder to the visitors that order is to be maintained and the rules are to be followed. Their residence is the Control Room, which is the first area one sees as he or she comes into the facility, and this uniformed staff can be an impressive sight.

Upon instructions from the Sergeant, the Officers make random dormitory searches, and uncover items that are considered to be contraband. Their finds have included items ranging from pens, unauthorized lotions, soaps, candy stashes to weapons and shanks. It is really not necessary for the residents to have shanks and it is sad that they may feel unsafe, because they are under supervision at all times. Things do happen within seconds, however, and they know only what they have learned in the streets, and at times they are afraid.

I remember one dorm search done by two of the Security Officers, and the items uncovered could have filled half of a grocery store. I saw the culprit contraband items piled up in the middle of the floor: hair mousse, hair gel, shampoo, conditioner, special Chinese crackers that are not easy to find, hot sauce, potato chips, four different kinds of cookies, liquorice, candy, beef jerky, cartons of juice, magic markers, pens, pencils, pads of paper, envelopes…the residents had stacks and stocks of more merchandise and supplies than I did. I have to admit that they shared some of the goodies with me; I'm sure it was not meant as a bribe for more phone time, but just sharing.

At times, my office became a haven for stockpiles of merchandise that are valuable in detention, such as gummy bears, Vienna Fingers and M & M's. I could have held the goodies as ransom, since they were locked in my office, but I didn't. The residents would come and make a withdrawal when they had a taste for a certain candy or cookie although they didn't fill out a withdrawal slip, but I teased them about making deposits and interest rates. One of my boys who had accumulated bags of candy, greeting and birthday cards and cartons of juice that he had earned from his commissary points, must have felt a pang of guilt at taking up space in my office with his bounty, since he suggested paying rent.

The residents have a commissary program and are permitted to have a number of items in their rooms, but this amounts to one hair product, one bar of soap, etc. It must be mentioned that the bars of soap were replaced by liquid soap, as a result of a bar of soap being put into a sock and used as a weapon.

We always have to remember where we are.

In detention, upon entry into the building and after clocking in, each staff member is assigned a set of keys and we used to be given a 'duress' as well. A duress is a heavy, alarm gadget that one can slip onto a belt or carry. If there is a situation or incident, one pulls a pin and the silent alarm would be set off in the Control Room, indicating which section of the building was in need. Security went running and the situation would be resolved.

For a long time, until the duress was discontinued, I had a running joke with the Sergeant who was giving out the agency keys. He would ask me if I wanted a duress for the day, and I would answer, 'No, I'm already under duress.'

It's good to start the day with a smile.

A Cinnamon Bun

It is generally common knowledge in most strata of society that the court system that serves society's members is overburdened; the calendars are overcrowded and the court personnel are busy to exhaustion. This complicated and difficult aspect of our society impacts on all those who are drawn into the long, meandering corridors of the courts, and the juveniles who are incarcerated in the detention system are no exception.

Many of the residents remain in detention on continued remands from their respective courts, awaiting a disposition on their cases, awaiting placement in a residential program or approval for a home-based program. Some residents are detained for six or eight months while this process lingers and inches forward very slowly. For most, it is a good experience and they mature and become patient while they wait.

One of my boys was in the system for seven months and was still waiting for forms to be signed, for approvals to be given and for those involved with him to determine which agency had the ultimate authority over his case and situation. He was in detention on a criminal charge, but his situation in detention was essentially beyond his criminal charge, since this youth had special needs. He had a lack of family support, as well as s lengthy history of family problems, leading him into the Child Welfare System, in which he had been spiraling much of his life. He felt neglected and alone. His family problems were not his fault, and he was feeling the results of an unfair system and a labored family situation.

After initially having a rough time when he was first admitted, he began to settle down and began to accept the attention and concern of staff. Initially, he had spouted negative and self-deprecating phrases, was depressed, and to him his future looked very hazy and vague. The system works very slowly, but it began to work for him as his mother began to resume a grasp on her life, with the help and support of caring others. Mother and son were on parallel paths, both regaining some measure of strength and self-esteem, both missing each other on many levels, and both finding each other again as the system finally kicked in for them.

My boy was slated for a residential program and was already calling it home, since he knew that he could not yet live with his mother who was still in the throes and processes of rebuilding and refurbishing her own life. He was due to go to court in the next few days, and he spoke to his mother on the phone. He knew she would be in court for him on the hopeful day and he knew that she had brought a change of clothing to the facility for him to wear in front of the Judge, to make a good appearance.

He told his mother on the phone, 'I have a good feeling that I'm going to leave this week for the program,' and he smiled. He then said to her, "Can you buy me a cinnamon bun and bring it to court with you? I love you too. I'll see you in court.' He hung up, turned to me and explained, 'I got locked up eating a cinnamon bun and I feel I'm going to leave eating a cinnamon bun.'

This gem of hope was from a youngster with special needs, who needed extra attention from staff and whose youthful days were missing the joy and fantasy of a child. He said that he had never heard of the expression, 'things in life go full circle,' but he had captured the essence of a life experience in a cinnamon bun.

Holidays

Holidays can be a stressful time in detention, both for residents and staff alike. During the holiday season, especially Christmas and Thanksgiving, talk shows, news stations and magazines all make sure to have time and space allotted for comforting messages. Most acknowledge that these family holidays may draw forth feelings of loss and loneliness.

The staff also experiences related feelings of frustration if they are obliged to work a double shift during these times, since detention is a twenty-four operation and each group requires two staff at any one time. The Administration acknowledges that children in detention require recognition of their feelings of loneliness and separation from family during these periods of time. Many of the residents are focused on their immediate predicament and have not yet developed the knowledge and maturity to realize that there will always be next Christmas and another Thanksgiving.

These holidays elicit familial feelings from the staff that the residents cannot receive from their own families due to their detention situation. The Food Service staff prepares the traditional Thanksgiving meal of turkey, sweet potatoes, cranberry sauce and all of the trimmings, and on Christmas, in addition to a similar dinner, each resident receives a gift which is placed in his property or sent home to his mother, and each dorm has a Christmas tree to decorate. There is also a giant Christmas set up in the yard, which is decorated and adorned by staff and residents. The Recreation Department provides decorations for each dorm, but much of the tinsel, glittering wrapping paper and holiday pictures are brought in by staff.

Halloween is a holiday during which the residents have some fun. There are no traditional family get-togethers or family meals to miss, there are no trees to light and decorate and there are no gifts to buy. There is not much to bring their spirits down. The only thing the residents may be missing is a lot of candy and cavities, and the possibility of getting into difficulty on the street during this holiday, which is replete with its own kind of potential trouble.

One Halloween, the residents on my dorm freed their imaginations with the common goal of winning first place in a decoration contest that was to be judged by several of the Administrators. The residents on the other dorms did their best and had the assistance of their staff, who hung pictures of ghosts, goblins, pumpkins and bats. The boys on my dorm did us all proud and enlisted the assistance of not only their own staff, but of the Housekeeping and Maintenance staff as well. They utilized all of their ingenuity and sent impulses along that special grapevine in the building to get extra sheets, extra old beat-up sneakers, oversized jeans and sweatshirts. Large garbage bags filled with leaves and twigs from the yard, provided by Housekeeping appeared on the dorm, and some of the residents started to create small flying ghosts and bats, which hung from the ceiling on strands of thread. There were about 150 small flying things swaying in the air currents in the dayroom of the dorm and large gossamer spider webs glimmered in the corners. The light fixtures were covered with red construction paper, converting the dormitory into a dimly lit, eerie room in which one could sense that scary things could happen at any time.

My boys went to work, creating additional residents on their dorm by stuffing the sweatshirts and jeans with sheets. They added socks and sneakers and stuffed the top of the sheet to create the head, topped off with a hat, and I suddenly had five more residents on my caseload. A large cardboard gravestone appeared with the letters R.I.P. inscribed on the stone, and the twigs and dried leaves were placed on the floor as if they naturally belonged to the netherworld of a graveyard.

Prior to the judging, I walked into the dormitory as I do many times during the day, and marveled at the realistic and impressive scene they had created with items that were gleaned from different parts of the facility. All of a sudden, one of the bodies that had been laid out in the 'graveyard' jumped up with leaves and twigs flying, and I in turn, almost jumped out of my skin. The residents started to laugh and the only thing I managed to say was, 'You got me...you really got me!'

The judges of the contest were escorted around to each dormitory by some ghostly residents who utilized the extra sheets to become apparitions, and they apparently got the same scary treatment I had received. They were also subjected to another surprise. Each dorm has a large, covered garbage can made of heavy plastic. After it was cleaned and sterilized, one of my smaller residents who was replete with a mask and a skeleton costume, hid himself inside of the can and jumped out as the judges entered the dorm, scaring screams from the startled judges.

Needless to say, my dormitory won first prize!

Friendships

It is generally accepted that when working with children or other clients in a counseling situation, the helper is not supposed to become too involved or attached to the helpee. It is truly important to maintain some measure of distance, maturity and professionalism with clients. This theory applies as well in detention.

However, detention is a situation and environment in which the staff is practically living with these children. We spend eight hours a day with them and become their surrogate parents. Their own parents tell us that they appreciate the work we do with their children and appreciate the fact that if they cannot be with them, at least they have concerned others who will act in their place.

Some of these children remain in detention for months, sometimes a year, a year and a half, or two years, going back and forth to court on their remand dates. They are waiting for some action to occur in court, for the D.A. to make an offer, for the witnesses to be located, for the police reports to be produced, for the court papers to be sent, and for many other pieces of the puzzle to be put in place in their cases.

We are taught counseling skills, group techniques, listening techniques, empathy and other skills that allow us to perform our jobs in detention. One of the basic skills that I learned is that we are supposed to use ourselves as a very basic tool when we work with our clients. It follows that when working with a child on a daily basis, for so many hours a day, every day for months and years, trust and friendships develop and grow. One does not lose that maturity and professionalism in dealing with the residents, but a few of the fences develop fishing holes through which one can drop a line, try some new bait and maybe pull up a deeper trust and support for our residents.

Two of my long-termers were sitting in my office one day. One was with us for a year and a half and the other for over two years. They had become friends and coincidentally, both of their cases were winding down, reaching dispositions. They were well known throughout the facility, were model residents and young men and had become very much at home with us. The impending change in their cases and status was unnerving for them. They felt safe and cared for in detention with their 'surrogate parents.' They were about to enter new territory, and would be leaving their comfortable, safe environment. One was getting all of his papers organized, leaving envelopes of his belongings in my office, getting ready to send them home. He had accumulated so much, and had such a variety of papers and projects because he had so many talents and interests. He was busy organizing while going through feelings of loss and was a bit melancholy due to his leaving and separation from us. We felt the same loss.

The other resident was reminiscing about his time in detention, how he had matured and changed, both physically and mentally, and about how fast the time had gone. Except for the reasons that had brought him to us, he said that he was glad to have had this experience. He said that he met so many good people here. I told my boy that when I first started this job, I was planning to use it as a stepping stone to go on to 'bigger and better things,' but I remained with the job because I realized that there was nothing bigger or better than working with them.

'Just think,' he said, 'If you hadn't stayed in the job, you wouldn't have met us.'

I agreed with him. It would have been a great loss.

Printed in the United States
By Bookmasters